WAKE UP, CHAMPION

Wake Up, Champion: A Radical Story About Redemption and a Game Plan to Level Up Your Life

© Copyright 2024 by Steve Weatherford

ISBN 13: 979-8-9878712-5-6

Printed in the United States of America

All rights reserved. This book is protected by the copyright laws of the United States of America. This book may not be copied or reprinted for commercial gain or profit. No portion of this book may be reproduced, stored in a retrieval system, or transmitted in any form or by any means—electronic, mechanical, photocopy, recording, scanning, or other—except for brief quotations in critical reviews or articles, without the prior written permission of Steve Weatherford.

Scriptures marked NLT are taken from the HOLY BIBLE, NEW LIVING TRANSLATION (NLT): Scriptures taken from the HOLY BIBLE, NEW LIVING TRANSLATION, Copyright© 1996, 2004, 2007 by Tyndale House Foundation. Used by permission of Tyndale House Publishers, Inc., Carol Stream, Illinois 60188. All rights reserved. Used by permission.

Scriptures marked ESV are taken from the ESV® Bible (The Holy Bible, English Standard Version, copyright© 2001 by Crossway, a publishing ministry of Good News Publishers. Used by permission. All rights reserved.

Scriptures marked NIV are taken from *The Holy Bible, New International Version®, NIV®*, Copyright © 1973, 1978, 1984, 2011 by Biblica, Inc.® Used by permission. All rights reserved worldwide.

Published by Turning Page Books

Editorial assistance by Phyllis Blanchard (phyllisblanchard.com) and Mike Yorkey (mikeyorkey.com)

Cover by Wes Briscoe and interior design by Emily Morelli (bluemusestudio.com)

To contact Steve Weatherford, email him at nextsteps@championsinchristministry.com.

SUPER BOWL CHAMPION, ENTREPRENEUR, HUSBAND AND FATHER
STEVE WEATHERFORD

WAKE UP, CHAMPION

A RADICAL STORY ABOUT REDEMPTION AND
A GAME PLAN TO LEVEL UP YOUR LIFE

*To my first and biggest hero, my dad.
Thank you for loving God with all
your heart, soul, and strength.
Thank you for loving my mom well.
Thank you for being a present
and faithful father to me.*

CONTENTS

A Note from Steve Weatherford.................................9

1. Super Bowl XLVI: A Meaningless Victory 11

2. Know Thyself to Lead Thyself........................... 21

3. Belonging..27

4. Wounds of Childhood....................................35

5. The Identity Chase......................................45

6. Become the Decathlete of Your Life 57

7. Relationship, Not Religion 69

8. Wise Men Take Baths 83

9. It's Time to Go Pro......................................89

10. Outfit the Launchpad with Your Time, Talents, and Treasures..................................99

It's Decision Time.. 111

Invite Steve Weatherford to Speak Today 113

A NOTE FROM STEVE WEATHERFORD

Each morning, when I wake up my oldest son, Ace, I whisper these words: "Wake up, Champion."

This is my way of giving him a sense of identity before he has any thoughts that morning. I am giving him permission to be great before he has any doubts. You see, it doesn't matter how many times you've been or felt like a champion because fear, doubt, and failure seem to work around the clock 24/7.

And that's why I am writing this book—to remind you of your greatness and help you discover, develop, and deploy God's greatest and best plan for your life. I'm praying and believing that the stories I share with you in *Wake Up, Champion* will recondition your mind, renew your heart, and light your spirit on fire to live a life of possibility that brings all the glory to God.

So, who am I to be giving you such wisdom?

I am a son of God, a husband, a father to six, a ten-year NFL veteran, a Super Bowl champion, an entrepreneur, an evangelist, a motivational speaker, and a legacy strategist.

From an early age, I found my identity in winning. This drive to succeed drove me to excellence in many areas. But because I was trying to find my identity in the world, nothing was ever enough. No championship trophy, no fitness magazine cover, no multi-million-dollar contract, or adoration of others could fill the hole I had in my heart—only God could do that. And I'm not talking about a *religion* with God . . . I'm talking about a *relationship* with God, which happened to me when I was thirty-six years old.

My prayer is that you find the same life-altering connection through these pages.

What will happen when you read this book?

First, *Wake Up, Champion* will help you identify the self-sabotaging patterns that are keeping you on the unfulfilling hamster wheel of life.

Next, I provide actionable steps to shift your thinking so you can let go of debilitating mindsets that are preventing you from living out God's true plan for your life.

Finally, I guide you through the practices of a mighty man (or woman) of God so you can get your house in order and *go pro* in life.

What you're about to read isn't just a wake-up call for someone who's unmotivated, confused, or stuck in their current circumstances with no way forward. Rather, *Wake Up, Champion* is your roadmap to recondition your mind so you can learn to think differently and adopt a new mindset that will allow you to walk in the fullness of who you are meant to be.

You've got gifts to develop and work to do.

It's time to wake up the champion in you!

1

SUPER BOWL XLVI: A MEANINGLESS VICTORY

I wouldn't call myself a gamer anymore, but there was a time when Super Mario Brothers was my magnificent obsession. I wanted to defeat the final boss, Bowser, to rescue the princess and save the world.

I was about seven years old when Nintendo was really popular. My mom and dad got my older brother, Chris, and me a console for Christmas one year, and it came with two games. Duck Hunt, that got old quick . . . and the holy grail of video games . . . the original Super Mario Brothers. My older brother and I played so many hours, taking turns falling in the lava and handing the controller over with a deep, frustration-filled sigh.

There came a time when it all changed . . . after many, many late nights and countless failed attempts (without cheat codes—a point of pride), I beat the game. I defeated the final boss; I achieved the ultimate goal; I saved the princess; I restored order to the kingdom. I remember the congratulatory screen saying:

"Thank you, Mario! Your quest is over."

Then it quickly cut to the credits . . . wait, what?! That's it?! My seven-year-old mind was blown. That's the finale?! I thought heaven would open up, and a beam of bright light would shine down. I thought maybe a messenger would immediately show up at our door with a trophy. I remember feeling so anxious with anticipation that something was gonna shift and be different when I defeated the game.

It didn't happen. The world tricked me. The advertisements, the video game magazines, the cartoons. They lied to me.

I thought the achievement would unlock something in my first-grade world; I was wrong.

Fast forward twenty years . . . and my Super Bowl experience was eerily similar.

Get comfy, friend. Let me explain.

It was February 5, 2012, Super Bowl XLVI (Roman numerals for 46), a true David-and-Goliath matchup, the 9-7 New York Giants taking on the highly favored New England Patriots led by the greatest football player to ever play, seven-time Super Bowl champion, Tom Brady.

This was my sixth year in the NFL as a punter, my fourth team, and my first trip to the biggest game in all of sports. Everyone that I loved attended the game. Mom, Dad, my brothers, and my sister. My grandma, my best friend—my wife, my wife's family, and my kids, not to mention the 124 million viewers at home.

I'll never forget how electric the morning of the game was. There were media trucks and reporters everywhere! It was a cold day in February in Indianapolis, Indiana, but that didn't stop football fans and curious onlookers from surrounding our team hotel and

SUPER BOWL XLVI: A MEANINGLESS VICTORY

blocking every entrance and exit.

Autograph seekers, young and old alike, were sardined into roped-off areas in the lobby. They would holler and call out each player's name as he walked out of the elevator. Each team member maintained focus straight ahead. We moved through the hotel lobby with liquid ferocity onto a fleet of Greyhound buses equipped with a battalion of Indiana State Police officers on motorcycles. Their assignment was to escort fifty-three gladiators into the arena for battle, where only one champion would emerge victorious.

I remember the stillness of the locker room before the game. Our quarterback, Eli Manning, quietly studied his playbook in a locker next to me while the linemen were in the far corner talking through formation adjustments and taping up all their injuries from the season. You could tell from the clubhouse atmosphere that this game was different.

"ALL IN!" our wide receiver Victor Cruz shouted. "All we need is all you've got!"

"ALL IN!" was a mantra our team adopted late in the regular season. It was created when our backs were against the wall and we were facing elimination. As a team, we put ourselves in a position that required us to win the last three games of the regular season to make it into the playoffs. This mantra challenged each member of the team to step up and do more. To prepare more, to study more, to be willing to sacrifice more, to be "ALL IN." I remember how the culture shifted when each member truly bought into that mindset.

Do you ever struggle with the fear of failure or the "imposter syndrome"?

I struggled so intensely with anxiousness, fear, and feeling overwhelmed that I vomited before every single NFL game I ever played in . . . you can ask any of my teammates. The crazy thing is, I wasn't the only player who dealt with the stress by regurgitating breakfast into a 55-gallon garbage drum on the sideline moments before kickoff.

It would blow your mind if you knew how many of your favorite musicians, athletes, and entrepreneurs struggle with the same doubts, addictions, and insecurities as *you*.

Finally, it's game time.

The Giants won the toss, and we chose to receive the ball. After the kickoff, our QB Eli Manning started out Super Bowl XLVI with an eight-play series of short passes and runs that eventually stalled out, resulting in our head coach Tom Coughlin deciding to punt from midfield. The goal was to trap the Patriots inside their own 10-yard line.

As the team punter, that was my job.

I remember jogging out onto the field feeling totally locked in, aware and prepared. The noise inside of Lucas Oil Stadium was deafening. I couldn't even hear my teammates making formation adjustments or audible alerts. The next thing I knew, the ball is snapped. I remember catching the snap, adjusting the ball, and sending the ball into orbit. End over end, the football soared near the dome ceiling. I remember as soon as it came off my foot, I could tell it was a good one . . . but I still held my breath. Wes Welker was the return man, and he was No. 1 in the league. He could change the game real fast.

As Wes Welker stood at the 8-yard line, he let the ball soar over his head. The oblong-shaped ball landed softly on the 2-yard line, bounced straight up into the air, and seemed to hang there—fluttering—as my teammate and long snapper, Zak DeOssie, caught it at the 4-yard line and handed the ball to the official.

I skipped off the field, pumping my fist in excitement. In my very specialized position on the team, that's as good as it gets. Except it got better on the next play when Tom Brady dropped back to pass and the pocket collapsed around him.

As you may remember, Tom ain't so mobile, and our All-Pro defensive end, Justin Tuck, smelled blood. As Tuck lunged at Brady, he chucked the ball down the middle. The only problem for Tom Brady and the Patriots was this: neither team had a soul within 25 yards of the pass he just threw. Yellow flags were thrown all over the field. The referee turned on his mic and motioned to the TV camera.

"Intentional grounding, New England Patriots. Result of the play is a safety. Two points, New York Giants."

The very next play after my punt was a safety for two points *and* we got the ball back. Talk about a swing of momentum for your team!

I had two more punts in the first half: both landed inside the 5-yard line. One of those punts was a 55-yard punt that landed out of bounds at the 2-yard line . . . I was having the greatest game of my entire life, in the biggest game of my entire life. I was in the zone, I was locked in, I was ALL IN.

I would later learn that during the halftime show, NBC commentator Chris Collinsworth said, "If I was gonna vote for an MVP right now, I'd vote for the punter Steve Weatherford." (True story.)

The second half went a lot like the first half. It was a showdown between two of the best coach-and-quarterback combinations the NFL has ever seen. If you give Pats head coach Bill Belichick enough time to make adjustments, he will defeat any adversary. And when you give him a quarterback like Brady, it's natural not to count your chickens before they hatch.

This game came down to the final ten minutes. The Patriots were up 17-15, and we had the ball at midfield, and our offense was rolling. Then a sack and holding penalty forced our offense to call on the punter one more time . . . God was guiding my foot and the ball on this day; I recorded another punt inside the 10-yard line.

This time, New England got the ball on the 8-yard line, which I later found out was a Super Bowl record that still stands today: most punts inside the 10-yard line.

We somehow held the Patriots and got the ball back for one last chance. Eli worked his magic and marched us down the field to put us ahead 21-17.

This was a street fight until the final play. It ended with Tom Brady throwing a 50-yard Hail Mary into the end zone as every Giants fan in the stadium froze in their seats while watching six-foot, seven-inch All-Pro tight end Rob Gronkowski leap into the air to snatch the game-winning touchdown. As the game clock hit zero, the ball was batted to the turf, and the New York Football Giants became World Champions!

I remember red-and-blue confetti falling down from the sky and thinking to myself, *Where is my family?* I spotted my wife; as I ran over to her, she handed me my four-year-old son, Ace. He said to me, "Dad, we did it, we won!" My heart melted to the floor. Two seconds later, I felt a tug on my jersey. I turned around. It was Al Roker, the longtime weatherman/interviewer on NBC's *Today Show*.

"Incredible game, Steve," Roker said. "How does it feel to be a Super Bowl champion?"

I wasn't shocked by the question—but I was surprised by *who* was asking me for a comment. My reply was, "Oh, man . . . you're Al Roker. I didn't know you knew my name."

Real smooth, Weatherford.

After fighting security to get my family and friends down onto the field, it was my turn to go up onto the stage and hold the Lombardi Trophy with my family for a photo. I remember my mom and dad's faces. I remember how shocked and proud they were.

After we showered, we all headed over to the team party at the hotel. It was the wildest hotel party I've ever been to . . . my poor parents. I think it was the first "rager" they've ever attended. They were appalled!

After two hours of hugging, fist-pumping, and laughing with teammates and families, the party died down, and one by one, the players and their families faded out of the celebratory festivities and back to their rooms. Even though I was a newly crowned world champion and would have loved to sleep in the same bed as my wife, rules are rules. The NFL teams rent out entire floors of hotels when we travel, but there was a strict *no females on the floor* rule. It was okay because I was exhausted and ready to shut it down.

I returned to my hotel room on the 17th floor, where I swiped my key card, pushed the door open, dropped my bag, and flipped the TV onto ESPN. Next thing I know, I hear muffled laughter and shouting from outside the hotel. I walked over to the window and looked down into the heart of downtown Indianapolis. At this point, it's about 2:30 in the morning, and to my shock and surprise, people were still out, laughing, hugging, taking group pictures with friends. All the people looked so happy. Then I realized the majority of those celebrating weren't even Giants fans. They were just folks happy to be near a place where something extraordinary happened.

I remember watching for a few minutes as I analyzed my own thoughts for the first time since the game ... this was my first moment of solitude. I vividly remember taking a deep breath in, and before I could exhale the oxygen from my lungs, a massive wave of depression came over me.

Here I am, sitting on top of the world ... I achieved my childhood dream. I did it in front of friends, family, and millions on TV. *Shouldn't I feel different? Isn't something supposed to shift or change in me?* The depression and anxiety hit me like an 18-wheeler. As my chest tightened, I realized everything I thought would be different was exactly the same.

This should have been a victorious, life-giving moment with a huge sense of accomplishment. I had played my best game ever on the world's largest football stage. I was a millionaire, had a beautiful wife, two kids, and tons of family and friends sharing in my victory.

But instead, I felt empty inside. I felt depressed. And that's when I realized: *Nothing changed!* I had to come to grips with the idea that a Super Bowl ring wasn't the be-all or end-all of my existence on this earth. I realized I was searching for things outside of me to fix something inside of me. What I was feeling wasn't an achievement or accolade issue; it was a mission, purpose, and identity issue.

At that moment, I knew there were no achievements inside of the NFL that would fill the God-sized hole in my soul.

The best and worst day of my life was the night we won the Super Bowl.

Have you ever felt like a promotion, an achievement, or a certain amount of income would make you feel different about yourself? I imagine that you are like me—an initial burst of pleasure and satisfaction followed rapidly by a feeling that says, *Is this all there is?*

Just like so many of us, I was searching for an extrinsic remedy for an intrinsic issue.

This defining moment in my life gave me the revelation that no award, paycheck, or trophy in the NFL would give me what I was searching for.

Take a moment to examine yourself and gain clarity on what matters most to you in life. Then, identify what is standing in the way of achieving that goal. For me, I was standing in my own way by operating *on mission* but not *on purpose*, which means that when I was chasing a lot of goals and things to build my own kingdom,

I became my own God. The missions were to serve me and me alone. But being "on purpose" means serving something bigger than yourself.

So, let me ask this pointed question: Is what you're chasing *on mission* or *on purpose*?

2

KNOW THYSELF TO LEAD THYSELF

Your uniqueness is your gifting. The only thing standing in between the ideal you have for yourself and the reality that you are in right now is a gap filled with lies, labels, and a skewed perception of what God created you to be.

It's like going to the carnival and standing in front of one of those fun house mirrors. The world does a great job of distorting reality by contouring our minds, polluting our thoughts, and stealing our hope. John 10:10 says the enemy comes to steal, kill, and destroy, but Jesus came so that He could give us life and why we're to give abundantly.

The reason I share this verse is because it's all about identity. Before the enemy kills or destroys us, he makes us weak. He made me weak as a little boy and stole my identity. When your identity is stolen, you don't know who you are. And when you don't know who you are, you don't know what to do.

Childhood for me was a time of serious disconnect between who I was and what I believed about myself.

My middle name, Thomas, comes from my maternal grandfather, Thomas Hobbs. My mom always said we were kindred spirits with the same personality and mannerisms. (She said I even walked like him.) Generous, loving, gregarious, energetic, and impulsive are some character traits my grandfather and I share.

Impulsive and energetic are lethal combinations for a kindergartner. It didn't take long for my teachers to realize I was going to be a problem. Rather than helping me to understand myself, they sent their problem to the principal's office, and the principal had a paddle for my problem. If it wasn't the paddle from the principal, my punishment was to sit against the wall and watch all the other kids run, jump, and play during recess. I was the one on the wall being punished during recess, wondering why I couldn't be "good" like the other kids.

I remember one afternoon when I was five or six and lived on the main road in a neighborhood in Greenwell Springs, Louisiana. That day, I thought it would be a great idea to see if I could run across the street before the next car arrived. So I made my way to the curb, where I hid and waited behind our mailbox. Then I looked to the left and right to see if any cars were coming.

A Ford station wagon with a mom behind the wheel appeared with several kids in the back. As this 5,000-pound car was barreling in my direction, I thought, *This is my shot. But don't make it easy on yourself, Steve. You need some competition.*

Crouched behind my mailbox in a three-point sprinter stance, I waited for them to get closer, so close that I wasn't sure if I could make it. At the last possible moment, I took off. As I dashed across the street, I heard the screech of the tires as the lady behind the wheel slammed on the brakes. I did it! I made it! Then I heard the shriek of my mother screaming my full name, "STEVEN!" When my mom used my full name, I really knew I stepped in it.

I turned around. The mom who'd slammed on the brakes rolled down her window. She was pissed. Well, not really pissed. I'm sure she was thankful I was alive.

"What do you think you were doing, young man? I could have killed you!"

"I'm sorry. I was just—"

Then, a new voice. "I'll take care of this."

My mother had arrived on the scene. The fire in her eyes told me I was in big trouble. But first, she had to square things away with the other mom.

"Ma'am, thank you for being alert. I'll handle this."

Mom grabbed me by the ear and marched me back into the house. I prepared myself for the whipping of a lifetime.

She sat me on the bed and pulled me into her lap, comforting me. "You scared me to death. What in the world were you thinking?" she asked softly.

"I knew I could beat the car, Mom. I just wanted it to be close."

This was a significant moment because it was the first time I remember receiving compassion versus punishment. I think this is also when my mom realized that my brain was wired differently and compassion was what I needed, not punishment.

This is when I knew I was different from the other kids.

At a young age, I was diagnosed with ADHD. Back in 1989, very few teachers and school administrators treated ADHD as an actual condition. They thought ADHD was a cop-out for a kid unwilling to sit still, follow the rules, and behave. It almost seemed like I had a daily meeting with the principal so he could re-remind me that I was not like the other twenty-six kids in my class.

"Grab your ankles, Steve," he'd say as he grasped a paddle. "Maybe this time you will learn your lesson."

I vividly remember coming home from kindergarten and crying in my mom's lap. I was frustrated at myself that I was different from the other kids. I began associating myself with being "different," as in "not good" and "not valuable." I started to hate who I was and looked at myself through a distorted mirror, nitpicking myself every chance I could, focusing on the 1 percent I did wrong versus the 99 percent I did right. I conditioned myself that way.

But that all changed when I met a man named Milton Clayton, who saw something special in me and made me feel like a treasure. Have you ever heard the saying: "One man's trash is another man's treasure"? Well, that's how Mr. Milton made me feel.

He was the father of one of the other kids I was competing against at a citywide interscholastic physical fitness competition where we competed in pull-ups, sit-ups, push-ups, and a one-mile run. Mr. Milton noticed I was different from the other kids, but not in a way that would make him want to take a wooden plank to my behind. I was different in a way that was good and excellent and worthy of praise. I could do things other kids who looked like me didn't have the capacity or capability to do.

Mr. Milton gave me a tryout invitation to join one of the best amateur track clubs in the entire country. I made the team and later went on to break a world record for my age group in the 800-meter relay.

I started to tie my self-worth to the results I created, the battles I won, and the records I broke. I remember all this athletic success being like a drug to me as a nine-year-old little boy.

"Steve, you are our MVP."

This felt so good to hear because I was desperate to be valued by others. A direct path for me to be valuable to others was to win early, win often, and never stop winning.

The Keeping Young track team had around two hundred athletes; many coaches were police officers, like Mr. Milton. The idea was to give kids—especially from minority neighborhoods—something to do and keep them out of trouble. Of the two hundred faces, I was the only white one, which earned me the nickname "White Lightning," which was much preferred to the alternative "Snowflake."

In addition to the relays, I competed in multi-events like the pentathlon. I later learned that Keeping Young sent nearly a half-dozen athletes to the NFL and lifted many others out of poverty because they went on to college, ran track, and got a quality education.

I share this story to illustrate the importance of alignments and identity. When my alignments shifted, the opinions of myself shifted, which in turn shifted my identity.

I didn't let my inability to be still stop me from going fast. I just needed the right person to give me an accurate reflection of who God created me to be, not a funhouse mirror reflection of myself.

Have you experienced something similar? Is there a disconnect between who you are and what you believe about yourself?

I suggest you take a long, hard look in the mirror and really own who you are and what you are not. Once you do this, you will receive peace and favor, and your God-given assignment will be revealed.

I've listed a few questions to help you better understand who you are:

- What about myself do I like the most?
- What about myself do I like the least?

- What are my fears?
- What are my gifts and/or unique abilities? (What comes easy or natural to you?)
- What is most important to me?
- What am I grateful for?
- What do I really want in this life?
- What motivates me?
- Who do I need to live the life I want?
- What aspects of my life do I wish to see a change in?

I urge you to write down your answers in a journal or notepad and think them through for a few days. Remember that your answers may change over time, but they are super important in the here and now.

3
BELONGING

Even more important than what you do in life is who you do life with. Unfortunately, most of us choose our friends/alignments based on what is available, not what is ideal. I use two filters to determine who I do life with:

- Do they value what I value?
- Do they have fruit in their life?

It won't be easy when you pursue the right alignment. There will always be a price to pay, but it will all be worth it.

In this chapter, I want to talk to you about one of the most cathartic moments in my life, but to do so, I need to tell you a little bit about my parents, Sam and Lisa Weatherford.

I don't know what kind of parents you grew up with, but my father and mother grew up in the church. They didn't have sex before they got married, they never smoked cigarettes, they didn't drink alcohol, and they really were who they said they were—in front of people and in the shadows. And I just assumed everyone else was the same.

While my dad was the spiritual leader in the household, my mom was the driving engine that made church a non-negotiable for my family. My mom was a Sunday school teacher and a Vacation Bible School teacher.

But because my parents (and my siblings) were so righteous, I had a hard time relating to them and didn't know if the *Jesus thing* was for me. I was not into worship music; I liked rap music. My parents wanted me to watch Christian shows like *7th Heaven*, but I wanted to watch *Rambo*. When we were driving and my mom played Christian books on tape, all I wanted to do was grab my GameBoy.

But what I loved even more than playing video games was professional wrestling. I lived for Monday nights when WWF's *Monday Night Raw* brought Randy Savage, Hulk Hogan, and the Ultimate Warrior into my living room. I cheered on my favorite wrestlers as they did crazy flips and acrobatic wrestling moves. Even better was when they beat each other with folding chairs!

When Mom saw how much I liked WWF, she bought me an Ultimate Warrior Stuffed Pillow Doll that was about three feet tall. I remember removing all the cushions from our couches and beds and laying them down in the living room so that I could jump off the living room couch and body slam this doll into the ground like one of my wrestling heroes. (Hulk Hogan was my favorite—a true American hero).

My sister, Carol, was six years younger than me—the perfect age for me to practice the Camel Clutch, a submission move made famous by the Iron Sheik. I'd wrestle Carol to the ground, sit on her back, squat and bring her arms over my thighs, apply a chin lock with an interlaced grip, and pull back on her head. It was a gnarly move.

Fortunately for my four-year-old sister, she was as pliable as Gumby.

On a hot summer night before my sixth-grade school year, my dad, who always kept an eye on my interests, took me to a strength exhibition event that changed me forever. The special evening took place at Comite Baptist Church in Baton Rouge, where I saw the Power Team in person. They were a group of men that I could finally relate to—tall, strong, and athletic. They believed in themselves, and others believed in them.

The Power Team weren't professional wrestlers but a medley of bulked-up, world-class athletes who performed amazing exhibitions of power, strength, and speed to spread the gospel and inspire kids to make positive changes in their lives. They bent rods of steel rebar, broke tall stacks of one-inch-thick concrete blocks with their hammer fists, tore telephone books in half, and caved in a pyramid of red bricks—blazing in flaming liquids—with their forearms.

This was *way* better than pro wrestling! My chin was magnetically glued to the stage, looking up to these guys in wonder.

With each robust demonstration of strength, loud cheers erupted from the several hundred kids and parents filling the church auditorium.

"Dad, I'm going up front."

My father nodded his okay, so I slipped into the first row.

The leader of the Power Team that night was Keith Craft, who stood six feet, six inches tall with 285 pounds of tan muscle and a broad 54-inch chest. He looked gargantuan and knew how to work a crowd.

"Let's make some noise!" he roared as other members of the Power Team blew into rubber hot water bottles, each breath inflating the device bigger and bigger. He got the crowd all crazy and hyped up as one hot water bottle exploded after another.

When the last hot water bottle had burst, Keith raised his hand to quiet the auditorium.

"I see that we have several of Baton Rouge's finest with us tonight." Keith waved his free hand toward the back. All heads turned to the rear, where two Baton Rouge Police Department officers stood in full gear, including sidearms. "Thank you, sirs, for your service. I would like to invite one of you to come onto this stage and handcuff me."

With great fanfare, the crowd watched intently as one of the cops made his way up the aisle and joined Keith onstage.

Keith extended his arms toward the officer. "I'm ready to be handcuffed," he said.

But first, a Power Team member wrapped Keith's wrists in silver duct tape while another held the microphone in front of his lips so he could continue his monologue. Then the policeman reached for a pair of stainless-steel handcuffs on his duty belt and slipped them over Keith's wrists. From the front row, just a few feet away, I could see that these handcuffs were real. I heard the click as they locked into place.

"Hey, you know what?" Keith said. "This is not enough for my God."

Turning to the Baton Rouge cop, he said, "I need you to bring me another pair of handcuffs."

Motions were made, and the second policeman came to the stage, where Keith was cuffed a second time.

"These are authentic Baton Rouge Police Department handcuffs, right?" Keith asked.

"Yes, sir," answered the first cop. "Plenty of criminals would attest to that."

"Well, I'm going to flex my arms and chest and upper body and push my body to the limit to break these chains, which are just like the chains of the devil," he announced. I stood transfixed as Keith strained against the handcuffs, his face contorted in pain as the heavy beat of rock music rose to a crescendo in the background. I could feel the tension rising.

"We have a God who is greater than our enemy, and He's greater than all the evil in the world," declared Keith, his face contorted from his efforts. "We don't have to fear Satan because Christ has already destroyed Satan's works on the cross. The power of God is greater than anything! Philippians 4:13 tells us that 'I can do all things through Christ who strengthens me.'"

Keith continued twisting and turning his wrists one way and another. The grueling effort turned his face beet red. "These are the toughest handcuffs I've ever worn," he managed through clenched teeth. "C'mon, everybody. Do you believe I can break these handcuffs in Jesus' name?"

"Yeah!" I yelled in unison with everyone inside the church.

"Then count down with me. Ten, nine, eight, seven..."

By the time Keith reached "one," the electricity in the crowd was palpable.

I watched Keith bend over from the strain. He squirmed for a few more seconds when—

—both sets of handcuffs flew off his wrists. Pandemonium swept the auditorium. I was knocked to the floor. Totally blown away.

When Keith broke off the handcuffs, he did not raise his hands and accept all of the adoration and praise like I saw the wrestlers do on TV. Instead, Keith did the opposite. He gave all the glory to God.

This was a paradigm shift to me, the first time I'd seen this dynamic combination of strength, vulnerability, and relatability.

As the crowd howled in delight, Keith turned to a new role: evangelist. He talked about how God wants excellence and abundance, how He wants us to grow and be stretched, and how He'll bring us to the highest mountains but always be with us in the lowest valleys. He said that if you want to break the spiritual chains in your life, there is only one thing—one person—who can do that, and that is through Jesus Christ.

"If you want to give your life to Jesus Christ and receive the assurance of eternal life with Him, then I invite you to come up here to become part of God's family," Keith said as he paced the stage. "Come to the front and accept Jesus into your heart as your Lord and Savior."

I was exhausted from screaming and cheering so much, yet I still had the strength to shoot both hands up into the air. I was already in the front row. That made me first in line, and I wasn't about to wait any longer. After his altar call, I responded and gave my life to Jesus.

I remember walking out of Comite Baptist with a feeling of hope—that a whole group of guys understood me, which meant that God understood me too. When I got home, I was excited to tell my mom about my experience at the Power Team event.

In my bedroom that night, I wrote down my new lifetime goals:

1. Become a Professional Athlete

2. Become an Olympic Champion

3. Be on the cover of *Muscle & Fitness* magazine

4. Become a father

I also came up with a wish list of items to search for at garage sales. I wanted sand-filled weights to develop my body, iron hangers to bend over my head in Jesus' name, and old magazines or newspapers that I could rip in half like Keith Craft and the Power Team did.

Seeing the Power Team gave me a whole new idea of what Christians could look like. Except for my dad, the only Christian men I had been exposed to were insecure, khaki-wearing dudes who drove busted-up minivans, tucked their shirts into their pleated pants, lived with below-average incomes, and didn't pay attention to physical fitness.

And then I was exposed to a new *Who*—with power, authority, kindness, gentleness, and compassion. I wanted what Keith had, so I did what he told me to do.

This was the first time I actually thought this Christian thing could work for me, that there were possibilities ahead, and that I belonged. From there on, everything started to click.

I believe God sent Keith Craft into my life as a divine appointment. I went from feeling like a reject, rebel, and a misfit to feeling like I finally belonged to Someone and something bigger than myself. That Someone was Jesus.

A fire of possibility was lit inside me, and I believed in my bones that if it were not for the exposure to those men and that event, I don't know if I ever would have received Jesus. I don't know if I would have gone all in on developing my body, developing my mind, and dreaming dreams that made my classmates, my teammates, and even some of my family members roll their eyes at my delusions of grandeur. The *who* that I was exposed to permitted me to dream about a new *what*.

My mom didn't have to tell me to read my Bible or say my prayers when I went to bed . . . now I wanted to read my Bible and kneel beside my bed to say my prayers.

Before moving on to the next chapter, I want you to write down a few of your life philosophies that you are currently living by and/or want to live by. These will be the frameworks that will drive everything you do and how you make every decision, both personal and professional. Think of them like a coffee filter: a lot goes in, but only the best comes out.

For example, here are a few of my life philosophies:

- **Your alignments determine your assignments.**

If you focus on the assignments, you'll miss the alignments. But if you focus on the alignments, the assignments will be revealed.

- **Amateurs make decisions based on feelings; pros make decisions based on commitments.**

When you listen to your emotions, you'll never push boundaries or leave your comfort zone. When you commit, you promise yourself that you will deliver, no matter what.

- **If you pay the right price, you get paid twice.**

Hard work is always rewarded. Working hard not only makes you strong and proud, but it grants you the confidence to be a winner in life.

What are your life philosophies? Don't have any? No problem. Take time to write them now . . . or use mine!

4

WOUNDS OF CHILDHOOD

THE BOOK OF JOHN IN the Bible talks about the different names of the devil . . . the enemy, the accuser, the deceiver, and the opposer. But notice that John doesn't call him the overcomer.

The devil doesn't have real power. He only has the power to persuade you, deceive you, and mislead you. The devil doesn't have the power to destroy you. The enemy's only hope is to use his power of persuasion to plant seeds of doubt inside you.

The most impactful night of my life was when I saw the Power Team and experienced God for the first time. I remember the peace I felt that gave me a deep, deep sense of belonging to God. I finally received grace for the things about myself that were different because those strong men assured me that God made me that way on purpose, for a reason. Hearing that made me feel special and loved.

I call this my honeymoon season with Jesus, very similar to a honeymoon with your spouse. In the following months, I let God change everything: my heart, my mind, and even my daily routine. It shocked my mom to see me read my Bible daily. I prayed to God every night without needing to be reminded. I wanted to talk to God—for me. I loved God, and He loved me back; that was the best summer of my life. And then, it was time to start seventh grade at a new school.

My parents had enrolled me at a Christian school in Baton Rouge, Louisiana. I was the new kid, but I was strangely excited about a fresh start with new friends, new teammates, and a brand-new identity—an identity in Jesus Christ. I was ready to take on the world because God was my daddy. He knows me and has plans for my life, I thought.

My new school was clean, nice, and filled with kind Christian students, teachers, and faculty. I loved my new school, and I especially loved my third-period teacher, whom I'll call Mr. Johnson. He was relatable, edgy, and cool. All the students loved him. He was such an encourager. Some days, I would walk into his classroom overwhelmed or anxious, but forty-five minutes later, I felt like I was seven feet tall and could overcome anything.

I loved the words of affirmation he would pour over me daily, like, "Steve, you really did a great job on your last paper. Great punctuation."

It felt really good to be praised for my efforts. I was used to being yelled at by teachers, but this guy was actually celebrating me, almost daily.

"Steve, I love having your smile in my class every day. You're such a joy to have around."

Hearing that praise made me feel so special.

Plus, Mr. Johnson constantly patted me on the back when he walked by my computer station. Without even saying a word, just with a touch, Mr. Johnson made me feel like he was proud of me.

But then, things got kind of weird.

The encouragement and affirmation turned into compliments

about my body. The pats on the shoulder turned into fifteen-second shoulder massages while I typed on my computer. The first time that happened, I froze. But then it made it less weird when I saw him do that to another student that same day. *Maybe Mr. Johnson is trying to help us relax and focus so we can do better work,* I thought.

This touch-here, touch-there continued a few times a week for several weeks. Then one day, he asked me to stay after class to give me some instruction. The class left pretty quickly as the bell rang. I remember getting up from my desk and grabbing my book bag, but then I felt Mr. Johnson hug me from behind. He wrapped his arms around my waist and hugged me while patting my stomach.

I froze . . . this was officially weird. I was lightweight freaking out. My mind was racing. Then Mr. Johnson said this while he rubbed my belly: "Wow, Steve! Your body is so strong. Do you have a six-pack under there?"

I couldn't speak . . . I couldn't move . . . my heart was racing . . . and there was no one around.

I think Mr. Johnson could sense how uncomfortable I was, but he still squeezed me like a dad hugging a son from behind and reminded me how special I was to him. I nodded and mumbled, "Thank you, Mr. Johnson." I slowly speed-walked out of there and into my next class before the bell rang.

That entire ordeal felt like it lasted for two hours, but it was likely less than ninety seconds because I still had time to make it to the next class, just in time to sit down. As I gathered myself, I tried to figure out if I was overreacting or if Mr. Johnson was a weirdo. In my mind, I was thinking: *No, not Mr. Johnson . . . he's your biggest supporter and encourager. You're probably just not used to that kind of love.*

I slowly rationalized what happened over the next few class periods.

I had almost forgotten about the incident entirely until about a week later when Mr. Johnson asked me to stay after class again, but he didn't mention that until right before the bell rang. My classmates fled out of the door while Mr. Johnson waited until the last student exited the classroom. When the coast was clear, he walked up behind me again with the same form and tact he used the last time.

He hugged me from behind and pushed his fully grown masculine frame into my ninety-two-pound prepubescent twelve-year-old body. He wrapped his arms around my waist and put his hands on my stomach, just like last time. But this time, he put his hands *inside* my uniform pants and underwear.

I went into total shock . . . I knew this wasn't right, but Mr. Johnson was a fully adult male a foot taller than me and outweighed me by a hundred pounds.

As he fondled me, he said, "Wow, you're pretty big. Do you like this, Steve?"

I couldn't answer. I was paralyzed with panic, muted by fear, and overwhelmed by shock.

I don't remember how long this abuse went on . . . maybe two minutes.

It's almost like my mind stopped recording memories for that short period of time . . . the next memories I recall are walking out of the classroom and Mr. Johnson saying to me, "This will be our little secret. You understand that, don't you?"

I didn't raise my head or say anything. I didn't know *what* to say.

He placed a hand on my shoulder. "If you tell anyone, no one will believe you."

I walked out of his classroom feeling like I was outside my own body, looking down at myself. I didn't know what was up from down. My world was closing in on me. I went to lunch next and asked a friend, "Does Mr. Johnson ever make you feel weird?"

"Not really. He's weird, but in a good way."

"Has Mr. Johnson ever touched you in a weird way?"

"Just his famous shoulder rub, but that's just what he does to all his students."

My friends could tell I was hiding something. "Why do you ask? What's up with you, man?" he asked.

"Has Mr. Johnson ever touched your privates?"

His eyes got big. "NO! Did he do that to you?"

I looked down in shame.

"Are you serious, Steve? You need to say something."

For the next two class periods, I deliberated what to do. I was scared and didn't know what to do. My biggest fear wasn't telling the principal; it was returning to Mr. Johnson's class the next day. The thought of returning to his classroom made my heart rate skyrocket, so much so that I started feeling dizzy. My chest got tight, and my breathing accelerated. I didn't realize it at the time, but I was having a panic attack.

I asked the teacher if I could go to the nurse's office. After she said yes, I bolted toward the nurse's office, sweating and out of breath. She measured my heart rate at 160 beats per minute and asked me two or three questions. I just exploded in tears... I told her everything. She calmly walked out of the room and returned with the school principal.

I walked the principal through what happened step by step. He left the room. I could hear him through the door, calling multiple people on the phone, but I couldn't make out what he was saying. Before I knew it, my mom and dad arrived and comforted me. I was in tears and so ashamed. I didn't want to repeat the story, so I let the principal talk to my parents alone in his office.

When we got home, my dad asked me if I wanted to talk about what happened. I absolutely did not. It wasn't until I wrote this book that my dad and mom heard the full story. I was so embarrassed and uncomfortable that I didn't want to talk about it ever again.

I assumed my principal informed my parents about everything, but that wasn't the case; my parents were only told that I was touched in an unprofessional manner, that the teacher had been fired, and that they were very sorry this happened. They didn't tell my parents that this teacher reached down into my pants and did things to me that should never have been done to a little twelve-year-old boy.

I never saw Mr. Johnson again. I heard he was escorted from campus, which opened the rumor mill. Word spread around the school like wildfire: *Mr. Johnson molested Steve Weatherford.*

My return was freakin' awful. Kids stared at me like I was this weird kid, but the junior and senior boys were the worst. They said the most hateful things to me.

If they weren't intentionally bumping into me while passing through the halls, I heard snide comments like:

What a liar.

How could you do that to Mr. Johnson?

You're just looking for attention.

The hazing was like stuff you see in the movies. I'd never been bullied like that before.

My parents asked me to stick it out until the end of the school year, another month away, so I did.

One evening, my dad came home from work and announced we were moving back to Indiana, where I had been born before we moved to the Baton Rouge area. I breathed a huge sigh of relief. Even though I'd miss my friends, I was ready for a change of scenery. I needed to be around people who didn't know what happened between Mr. Johnson and me.

The move helped give me a fresh start, but it did not heal the damage that had been done. I pretended that everything was okay when, in actuality, I was masking my true emotions and really struggling with questions that needed to be answered. The trouble is that I didn't feel like there was anyone I could talk to. My dad was and is a great and faithful father, and I certainly honor him, but I don't think my father was equipped to deal with helping his son navigate sexual molestation and all the trauma, addictions, and coping tactics that followed.

I was struggling with questions like:

- "If God is so good, how could he let this happen to me."
- "If God loves me, why didn't He protect me from this perverted man who stole my purity, ruined my mind, and made me feel dirty and unlovable?"
- "Does this make me gay now?"

When those questions didn't get answered, I turned my back on God and decided to do life on my own. I realized I was small and weak, so I committed to changing what I hated about myself. I focused on things I could control, like lifting weights and playing sports. I stayed busy with games and contests so I didn't have to feel the pain. I found that when I was competing, I was able to escape into an alter ego and set myself on a new mission. I found myself proving my worthiness to the scoreboard time and time again. I became obsessed with whatever goal I set for myself, constantly searching for a bigger and better dopamine hit to mask the pain that was inside me.

I stopped reading my Bible and talking to God because I was angry at God. I was doubtful He existed. And then the next bomb dropped on me. In the same school year, I was introduced to pornography when my friend gave me a VHS tape. I knew it was wrong to watch all those naked bodies. But it was so exciting, and the pleasure it gave me was a drug that my young brain became addicted to. Watching that porn tape became my secret way of dealing with my depression and loneliness.

So, let's count things down here: inside the span of twelve months, I received Jesus, survived sexual abuse, and secretly found pornography. No wonder I was a confused twelve and thirteen-year-old. I had no idea who I was or that the devil roams around like a roaring lion (1 Peter 5:8). To be honest, my identity was as fragile as my belief in God.

I wish someone would have told me that God does *not* author sexual abuse, cancer, or murder. That our God doesn't *want* to see us suffer with disease, divorce, or death, but just the opposite: the only plans God has for us are good plans.

In Scripture, His Word says:

> "For I know the plans I have for you," declares the Lord, "plans to prosper you and not to harm you, plans to give you hope and a future."
> JEREMIAH 29:11 (NIV)

> The Lord is good,
> a refuge in times of trouble.
> He cares for those who trust in him.
> NAHUM 1:7 (NIV)

> And we know that in all things God works for the good of those who love him, who have been called according to his purpose.
> ROMANS 8:28 (NIV)

These are some of my favorite verses because they are so clear and plain. They are promises from God for you and me. They say that God won't let anything happen to you that won't be used for good.

When I was less mature, I couldn't fathom how God could use death, disease, or abuse for "good." But now I see how He used my scars to help other men and families heal every day.

Whenever I take the stage to teach, speak, or lead, I share this vulnerable part of my story.

There is nothing masculine about being molested. But the healing that took place afterward was supernatural and never fails. Every single time I speak from the stage and share my story, I have at least one person waiting for me by the exit because he or she has a strange prompting to share something with me that they've never shared with anyone else.

Y'all thought I loved rocking the stage!? Nah, that's my second favorite part . . . I live for the personal one-on-one breakthrough with God's sons and daughters. I can see the pain and depression in their eyes disappear as they bring the mold out of the darkness and into the light.

> "I show my scars so that others know they can heal."
> AUTHOR RHACHELLE NICOL'

Dramatic events that happen to us at a young age can haunt us well into adulthood. The memories and the feelings associated with those memories live inside us until we fully bring them to light and set them free.

Secrets like these love to live in the dark, like mold loves to live in the basement. The problem with secrets and mold is that they're toxic to everyone and everything around. There is only one solution to solve them both—bring them to light!

We are not supposed to carry burdens, so I want you to identify them right now. Write down three defining moments (such as disappointments, failures, hard times) that impacted you at a young age . . . moments that you feel changed the trajectory of your life.

Maybe you didn't have something super dramatic happen to you, but perhaps there was a time when your dad didn't pick you up from school and you felt abandoned, something like that. Or maybe your parents divorced, or you lost a parent or a sibling.

1.

2.

3.

After writing down your three defining moments, take a moment to think about how God used those instances for good. Romans 8:28 (NIV) says, "And we know that all things work for the good for those who love him, who have been called according to his purpose."

Take some time to reframe your thinking and associate the positive to each of your defining moments.

5
THE IDENTITY CHASE

EVERY ADVERSITY IN OUR LIVES can be a roadblock that shuts us down or a stepping stone that leads to growth and advancement, which leads me to this question:

What is the common denominator of high achievers, pro athletes, and CEO leaders?

Answer: it's how great they are at overcoming adversity.

Overcoming adversity comes down to one thing: having a clearly defined identity, which is how you view yourself. Identity is the place where decisions are made and is comprised of five parts:

- core values: what matters most to you
- beliefs: what you think is possible
- experiences: what you know to be true
- strengths: what comes naturally to you
- weaknesses: what is difficult for you

Your upbringing, your relationships, and your perspectives heavily influence your identity, which acts as a guiding compass, providing you with a sense of direction, inner strength, and resilience. When you go through life events that you can't understand, you begin to doubt things that used to be certain.

The enemy loves to take our painful experiences to increase doubt, distraction, fear, and confusion. The enemy also loves it when we try to build our identity in the world, which is exactly what I did for the first thirty-six years of my life. I scratched, fought, and clawed for achievements, accolades, appreciation, and affluence, building my identity in the world and of the world.

What you are about to read in the coming chapter showcases the season of my life where I focused on myself. I was wounded. My identity was broken, but I decided I wanted to change that. I made it up in my mind that if I became strong, successful, and famous, I would feel better about myself. I would be "happy."

I was 100 percent focused on my mission to become a pro athlete with a bodybuilder's body. I didn't care how I got there and never asked myself the million-dollar question: *Why?*

Looking back on this period of my life, so much of my drive to succeed came from a place of pain, suffering, and lack of appreciation. I had a broken identity and was searching for the things of the world to fix it.

"We're moving," my dad said one evening while we ate dinner. "I got a great job opportunity in Terre Haute, Indiana. We're moving this summer."

This announcement came two months after the incident with Mr. Johnson. Most thirteen-year-old boys would be sad to leave their school, their sports teams, their church, or their best friends, but not me. I started packing up my room that night. I needed a fresh start in the worst way. I decided I was going to leave all my problems in Baton Rouge.

I was so excited about moving to a new place, where I'd go to a new school, have new classmates, try out for new sports teams, and enjoy a whole new beginning. A place where no one knew my past, where I could be anyone and anything I wanted to be.

I knew I needed to do one last thing before the moving van arrived, however. I waited until my mom and dad were busy with my older brother, Chris, and younger sister, Carol. Then I grabbed my secret porn stash, rode my bike to the gas station, and threw all the magazines and videos in the trash can, promising myself, "Never again."

Even though I was mad at God, I still had a really strong conscience. Every time I would engage in the excitement of watching others have sex, massive amounts of guilt and shame would quickly follow it. I'd say to myself: "I'm not gonna do this again ...." Then, a few weeks later, I'd find myself in my bedroom with the door locked, looking at naked bodies again.

I now know that staring at those images caused euphoric releases of chemicals called dopamine (the "feel good" neurotransmitter) in my brain. The same neurotransmitter is released when you engage in other activities like gambling, overeating, social media, or drug use. Dopamine doesn't just respond to negative stimuli like drugs, but we can also achieve dopamine release through healthy hobbies like exercising, praying, learning, or socializing. I caught onto this as a young boy when I felt the dopamine hit after performing well on the sports field.

I played four sports at Terre Haute North High School, but it was the strength of my kicking leg that enticed the legendary varsity football coach, Wayne Stahley, onto the soccer field in search of this skinny sophomore kid on the soccer team with a rocket launcher for a right leg. Our varsity football team needed a field goal kicker.

Football was a huge deal in Terre Haute. Our small city had about 50,000 people at the time, but it wasn't unusual to draw a crowd of over 10,000 fans for our crosstown rivalry game—Terre Haute North versus South.

It's hilarious looking back at my pictures from my sophomore year. I was so skinny that when you put a white football helmet on my head, it looked like a golf ball on top of a tee. I was a wiry 108 pounds soaking wet. I didn't have much upper-body strength, but my right leg had more snap than Indiana Jones's bullwhip.

My kicking career didn't start on the right foot, so to speak. I was so nervous and felt insanely uncomfortable going through all the warm-up drills at the start of practice. I'd done high knees and butt kicks hundreds of times, but never with twenty pounds of pads and a massive helmet on my head.

The next thing I knew, I heard a whistle blow with Coach Stahley calling for a field-goal attempt. Before that happened, Coach gathered the team and introduced me as the new kicker. "I know he doesn't look like much, but he's got a cannon for a leg," the coach said.

The biggest guy at my school was Mike Canada, who ran things at our campus. He was a six-foot, four-inch, 275-pound round belly, tobacco-chewing (while at football practice) badass. He was also my long snapper for a field goal attempt. And my holder was our star quarterback, Chris Farr, the most handsome and popular guy at my school.

So, I had the toughest guy at North and the most popular guy in my entire school staring at me, waiting for me to nod so they could snap the football and see if the new kid would live up to the hype. With the rest of the team anxiously watching, I vividly remember Chris Farr yelling, "Hut, hut." I see Mike Canada fire the ball back. The ball gets placed down on the kicking tee. I swallow the lump in my throat and charge that football like a 108-pound raging bull.

THE IDENTITY CHASE

Then I swung my leg with everything I had.

I heard a resounding thud as my size 9 Adidas shoe hit the pigskin. I know I hit it straight. I know I hit it hard—but the football never got more than three feet off the ground! The very next thing I heard was a loud *smack*. I lifted my head and peeked through my facemask to see Mike Canada jumping up from his stance and grabbing his right butt cheek in howling pain.

My first field goal attempt with the varsity ended up being an unwanted football enema for my long snapper, Mike Canada, who chased me off the field and told me never to return.

My life is over, I thought. I wasn't even worried about my football career. To make amends, I showed up the next day with five cans of Copenhagen chewing tobacco as a peace offering to Mike. Thankfully, he let me back on the team, and my kicking career began the following Friday night. In my very first varsity game, I hit a 49-yard game-winner.

Kicking the football was a skill that came to me very naturally. As a soccer player, I felt like kicking field goals was easy. The ball wasn't moving, and the posts I needed to kick the ball through didn't even have a goalie.

I got a lot of attention during my first season. I remember walking down the hallway, proud to wear my varsity jersey to school on "Game Day" Fridays. Thank God my mom was handy with the sewing machine because my jersey was too big on me. She had to sew elastic into the sleeves so I could fill my jersey out like the real football players on my team.

I became obsessed with the weight room when I started playing football. I clung to the words of childhood hero Bruce Lee, the martial artist and actor: "Fear not the man who has practiced 10,000 kicks once," he said, "but fear the man who has practiced one kick 10,000 times." This quote speaks to mastery over a skill. Mastery gives you authority, and authority makes you valuable, which I was desperately seeking.

Through maniacal dedication to training, nutrition, and recovery, I unlocked my athletic potential at North High. I grew from five-foot-nine to six-foot-three, gained over one hundred pounds, earned thirteen varsity letters in four sports, and received multiple college athletic scholarship offers across multiple sports. As I achieved these accolades and built my body, I was also battling a quiet but constant internal struggle with myself. Something was missing even when I decided to go to the University of Illinois on a full-ride offer.

I remember my high school and college years being filled with checking boxes of achievements that would "unlock" fulfillment, peace, or joy inside of me that wasn't available until the achievement happened. Looking back on everything now, I'd say my life was just like Super Mario Bros. on the Nintendo: I was moving from level to level, hoping that the next level would fill a void inside me. So much so that I decided that playing football for Illinois in the Big Ten wasn't enough. I joined the Fighting Illini track team and competed in the decathlon with the dream of one day becoming an Olympian, working hard and even breaking the school record to become All-Conference in track my freshman season.

Each year at Illinois, I improved in almost every category as a punter. Some of my fondest memories were spent training in the stadium with my girlfriend and now my wife, Laura. When we started dating, I was very clear with her: my goal was to go to the NFL. I told her if she wanted to spend time with me in the summer, then she needed to be willing to train with me because that was my top priority. She quickly learned to underhand toss the football to me, which simulated a snap. We spent hundreds of hours working together to master the craft and skill of punting. For instance, I worked on mastering a punt for hang time. Mastering a punt for direction, a punt for windy games, and a punt to force a fair catch. Laura helped me to take an ordinary skill and create mastery in it. I later proposed to her on the 50-yard line in Memorial Stadium on the Illini campus in Champaign, Illinois.

After finishing my senior football season at the University of Illinois, I was one of the nation's top-ranked punters, and the NFL was looking like a real possibility. After the NFL Combine and several private workouts, I signed a contract with the New Orleans Saints as an undrafted free agent. I was going to compete against their current punter, Mitch Berger. He was a ten-year vet, a Pro Bowler in the prime of his career. Even though I was an explosive young talent, I was going to need a miracle to take this guy's job because in the NFL, teams only keep one punter—there are no backups. You're either a starting punter in the NFL, or you're jobless and on the streets. There's no in between.

On the very first day of training camp, Mitch hurt his groin, and for the next four weeks, I balled out. I was hitting 60-plus-yard punts in every single preseason game. Mitch kept having issues with his injury. On cut day, I waited by my phone in my dorm room, praying it would never ring because if a coach calls you, that means your dream is over.

My phone never rang. The next morning, I walked into the team facility to check the final roster, just to be sure I made the team. As I stepped into the locker room, I noticed my locker had been cleared out and the piece of tape that read "Weatherford" had been removed. I panicked. Did I get cut? Did they forget to call me?

Then I noticed someone had placed all my stuff inside a *new* locker with a permanent nameplate bearing my name.

Here's what happened: NFL locker rooms usually make the locker placement numerically to make it easy for the equipment staff to know where to put players' laundry and equipment between workouts. Because I was number 7, my new locker was wedged between our running back Reggie Bush at number 5 and our quarterback Drew Brees at number 9. I thought to myself: Is this real life? I quickly pulled out my phone to call my dad.

"Dad, they are stitching Weatherford on the back of the number 7 jersey right now. It's official. I made the team. I'm a pro."

I think I was expecting the heavens to open up and a light shine down on me as my father said, "Well done, son. I'm so proud of you."

My dad replied in a much more practical manner. "Don't forget your contract isn't guaranteed," he said. "Your contract is week to week."

Although my dad was speaking truth and wanted to keep me focused and grounded, I wanted to hear my dad say, "I'm so proud of you."

Now, let's get one thing straight: my dad was and is a great dad, a faithful man, a steady figure in my life, but he doesn't use fluffy words or blow smoke. If you haven't noticed yet, words of affirmation are a love language for me. My dad grew up with an old-school dad. You know—the strong, silent type who doesn't show emotion or communicate well.

I don't have any memories of my grandpa smiling or laughing. My dad wasn't like that; he was engaging but rarely silly. I didn't grow up with a dad who talked about his feelings or fears. I don't ever remember talking to my dad about *my* feelings or fears, but I definitely viewed my dad as a "real man." Even though he wasn't a mountain of a man like my childhood hero, Hulk Hogan, Dad could do anything. He built our childhood home, coached our sports teams, knew how to hunt, could fish, change the oil, and even led a Bible study at my church.

My dad was respected by men at church and his colleagues at

work. My dad gave me a great example of what a devoted husband, committed father, and Man of God looked like. To this day, I still have never seen my dad break character. I've never heard my dad curse, lie, cheat, or steal. My dad has shaped who I am more than any other man. He taught me the core values of grit, commitment, humility, and faithfulness. My dad taught me that Weatherfords don't quit. My dad taught me nothing comes before God, and family is everything. Above all things, I knew my dad's identity was firmly planted in Christ. He had a strength and peace in his spirit that can only come from a deep and meaningful relationship with God. That was his X-factor, but I didn't realize this until my NFL career was over.

For the next ten seasons, I continued to look out into the world, thinking that the next award, paycheck, trophy, or accolade would fill the hole in my soul. I didn't realize the hole was something only God could fill.

Being nominated for the Walter Payton NFL Man of Year award given to the League's most philanthropic player wasn't enough, so I thought maybe becoming the Fittest Man in the NFL would do it. Or splashing my six-pack physique on the cover of *Muscle & Fitness* in thirty-seven countries. Or becoming a Super Bowl champion might complete the journey. As everything was changing around me, nothing was changing within me.

I transformed the pain and trauma of what I experienced at a young age into a surgical and disciplined focus. I developed my abilities and learned how to execute at the highest levels, and I did whatever it took to achieve the four goals I wrote down when I was thirteen years old. At the end of the day, I am proud of that little boy for being able to do that, but my heart hurts because he never got to enjoy the journey. I was too focused on moving to the next goal, the next mission, the next target, and the next objective. I was living my life on a mission, but I was off purpose.

On September 4, 2015, I released a statement through a YouTube video announcing my retirement while thanking my coaches, friends, fans, and family for all their support.

I instantly accepted several TV/radio opportunities, thinking, praying, and hoping whatever came next would be the thing I was looking for . . . that I would be onto the next "mission."

A monk and theologian, Thomas Merton, said it best: "People may spend their whole lives climbing the ladder of success only to find, once they reach the top, that the ladder is leaning against the wrong wall."

I realized my life ladder was leaning against the wrong wall. It was time for drastic and swift changes, as I'll get into in my next chapter.

Have you ever found yourself taking your identity from the job you have? What results you create? The home you live in? The car you drive?

One of the most powerful things you can do is to disconnect yourself from the "scoreboard of life." How often do you draw your internal value from an external result?

That is exactly what keeps us in the perpetual loop, so I want you to get out of the matrix the way I did. If your life feels like an endless to-do list, and even when you complete the list, there are times that don't bring peace, then it's time to get clear on who you are. Let me help you jump-start the process of defining your identity more clearly.

Take some quiet time to answer questions that will help you gain a bird's eye view of who you are and your current identity. If you don't like what you see, now is the perfect time to change your trajectory!

Let's start here:

- Your core values: What matters most to you?

Remember, these are traits, not things like generosity, integrity, discipline, honor, growth, excellence, and joy.

- Your core beliefs: What is true?

God is real. God is good. God has plans for our lives. Marriage is a covenant. Money is a tool. Family is a blessing. Children are a gift. Jesus is the way. Healing is available.

- Your experiences: What is possible?

A collection of your life-defining moments subconsciously controls what you think is possible. What are some of those defining moments? I'd like you to write down some of your good moments and bad moments. We typically have around three defining moments per decade of life.

I'll tell you one of mine: being five years old and getting spanked for not sitting still. What that defining moment taught me is that being hyper is bad . . . and I was bad.

Another was when I was eleven and received Jesus at a Power Team event. What that defining moment taught me is that my uniqueness was created on purpose by God. I belonged to God. I was forgiven. There was joy and peace in Jesus.

Then, there was the sexual abuse that happened when I was twelve years old. I thought, *I'm dirty, I'm broken. I can't trust men. God isn't good.*

- Your strengths: What comes naturally to you?

Ask three people closest to you what they think your strengths are. I know mine: physical authority/athleticism, encouragement, enthusiasm, vision, and communication.

- Your weaknesses: What is difficult for you?

Is it organization, punctuality, details, planning, patience, ego, or humility?

If any of these traits fit you, then know you're not alone.

6

BECOME THE DECATHLETE OF YOUR LIFE

THE TITLE "WORLD'S GREATEST ATHLETE" is given to the Olympic gold medalist of the decathlon, a ten-event contest covering a wide range of athletic disciplines over two days.

The key to winning the decathlon and becoming the most well-rounded athlete walking the earth isn't training to become the fastest runner, the best shot putter, or the highest pole vaulter. Instead, the prize is awarded to the athlete with no gaps—who scores many points in every event. He's the one who can do it all, not win it all. This is why he is called the World's Greatest Athlete.

Focusing on one area of excellence creates gaps and holes in other areas of your life. Instead of beating yourself down day in and day out to become the best in your profession, remove the blinders, enlarge your identity, and realize you were created for more. Take aim to become the decathlete of your life.

This perspective shift will be a game-changer, especially when you realize success or legacy is achieved through your body of work, not in one area of life. Don't be the one who wins the world but loses his or her soul or the person who gains a city but loses his or her family.

My retirement from the NFL came as a shock to a lot of people, including my mentor, NFL veteran placekicker John Carney, who played for twenty-three seasons.

I remember John calling and trying to talk me off the edge of retiring. He did so because he knew what life was like on the other side of the NFL. There is no roped-off VIP section, no more free travel or food, and no more preferential treatment when you are a retired NFL memory.

But John didn't realize I wasn't looking for an easier or better life; I was looking for a more meaningful and purpose-filled life. In my desperation, I just couldn't see myself finding that in the NFL. I knew another Super Bowl or Pro Bowl wouldn't plug the God-sized hole in my chest. I was sure my fulfillment lay elsewhere, so I trusted my gut and hung up my cleats.

Quickly moving into what I thought would be my next career path—working in the media—I accepted a job with ESPN to co-host a radio show with my friend Dave Rothenberg, a sports talk radio host. I also hosted a show on Spike TV and did other sports commentary for various radio and TV stations.

I was a guest on "The Dr. Oz Show," "Good Morning America," and "Shark Tank." While being on TV was a natural progression for me, I realized something fairly quickly: I was talking about things that really weren't important to me. Being part of the media landscape became unfulfilling in the same way that the NFL had become. On top of that, another issue was at play: my wife, Laura, was really, really ready to get out of New York and

New Jersey and move to San Diego, where we had lived during my NFL off-seasons. She loved the sunny climate, sandy beaches, and outdoor shopping.

I was ready for a change too. We decided to move back to America's Finest City in early 2017, where I planned to start my own podcast and talk about topics I felt passionate about—like fitness, business, and personal development with my amazing friends as guests. At least, that was the general idea.

We leased a beautiful home in Rancho Santa Fe, the nicest part of San Diego with manicured, Spanish-style homes on three-acre parcels. After moving into a gorgeous property, however, we discovered that the refrigerator and stove didn't work.

It took more than a month for the appliances to be replaced. In the meantime, we ate out nearly every meal. I gained fifteen pounds eating restaurant food, and it wasn't a good fifteen pounds. I hit the scales at 253 pounds, the most I ever weighed in my life.

Let's just say it would be hard to talk credibly about the importance of being fit when I was more round than hard. I knew it was time to get my life together and my body back in shape. I started my health comeback by having my blood and urine tested to see where my metabolic markers, hormones, and cortisol levels were. I sat down with a team comprised of a nutritionist, a kinesiologist, and a hormone specialist. They helped me map out a plan for training, meals, supplements, recovery, sleep—every single part of the game. And then I went to work!

The entire time, I shared my journey on social media, saying, *Guys, this is the biggest I've ever been, but here's what I'm doing about it.* Every meal, every exercise, every rep, every supplement, when I did it, why I did it, and how I did it—I talked about it all.

I jump-started my transformation with a five-day detox period to reset my metabolic rate and followed with a strict diet that curbed my carbs and included different probiotics, fatty acids, and a cleansing green juice.

Ten days in, I received a call from my friend Matt Tuthill, an editor at *Muscle & Fitness* magazine. "I see what you are doing on social media," he said. "My CEO wants me to do a story on your transition from an NFL star to a fitness icon now that your football days are over."

Fitness icon? I was a soft and huggable 250 pounds, but Matt didn't know that. He was wondering if I could do a photo shoot in Las Vegas in thirty days. He and several other *Muscle & Fitness* editors would be there as well, attending a fitness convention.

"If the photos turn out great, we're slotting you for the November cover," Matt said. "No guarantees, but this time around, I think it'll stick."

A couple of years earlier, Mark had written a story about me entitled "Steve Weatherford Is the NFL's Fittest Man," which was slated for the cover of the June 2015 issue. At the last minute, the editors bumped me off the cover for Arnold Schwarzenegger, who had a new *Terminator* movie coming out.

"Got it," I replied. This was another chance to fulfill a lifelong dream, which inspired me to focus on what I needed to get done.

For the next month, I buckled down and followed my nutrition, supplement, and exercise plan to the letter. I shared everything I was doing on Instagram, along with posting YouTube videos. I wanted everyone to see what I was doing.

The grind and the sacrifice resulted in a huge success. My love handles melted away, and my six-pack once again revealed itself. I felt like a spartan when I stepped before a white backdrop in a Las Vegas hotel room and heard the clicks from the freelance photographer. This time, I did end up on the cover after being shot by the best fitness photographer in the world, Per Bernal, who has become a good friend.

BECOME THE DECATHLETE OF YOUR LIFE

The results speak for themselves:

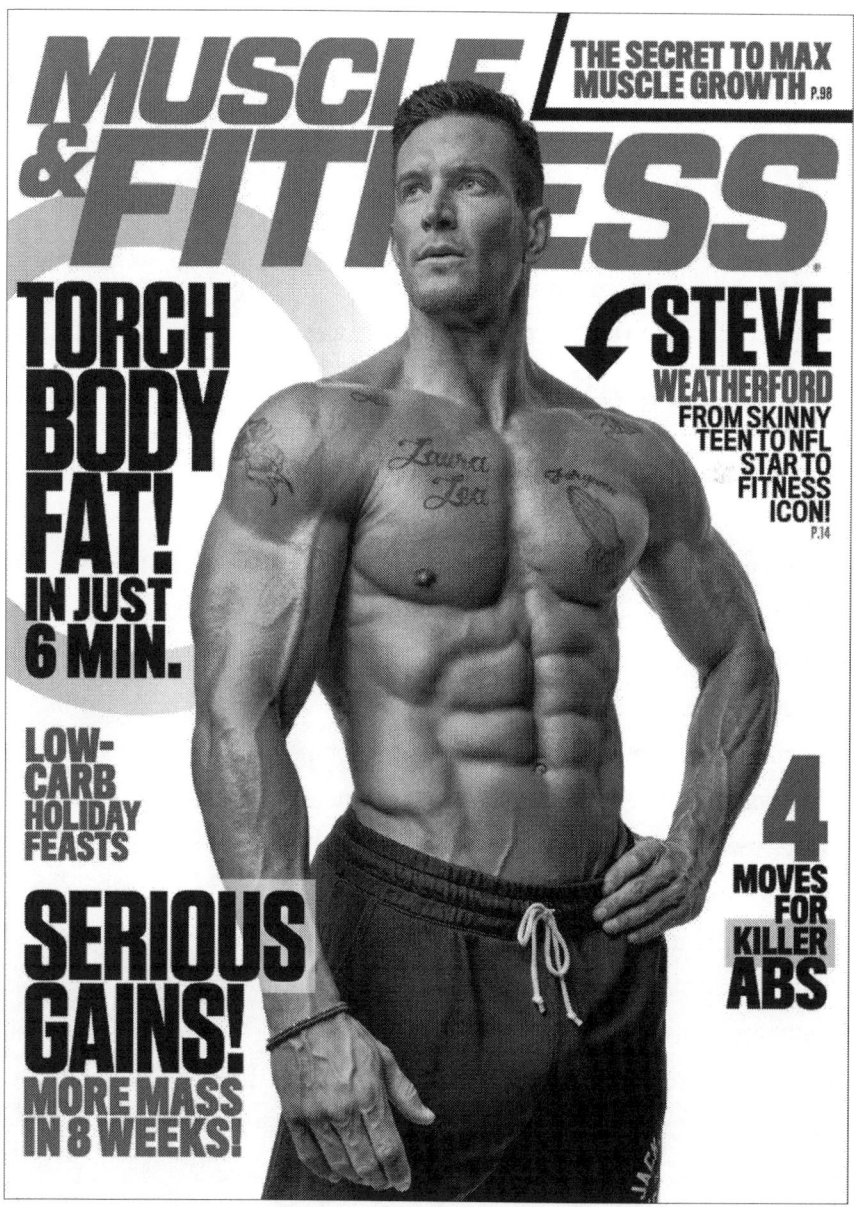

While sharing what was happening on social media, I began receiving hundreds and hundreds of private messages on Instagram and Facebook, each saying roughly the same thing:

Hey Steve, would you put together everything you just did in a little plan? Just tell me what supplements to take, what foods to eat, and what workouts to do. Make it easy for me.

A light bulb went off. There were tons of people who wanted to turn their health around and wanted me to tell them what to do and what to buy. And since they needed to purchase supplements, why not buy them from me?

I decided to launch my own nutritional supplement business and hired a coach/mentor to help me maximize my efforts. I found a company to produce what I needed and announced what I was doing on social media—and was blown away when I received $479,000 in orders in only four days! I called the program the Metabolic Reset.

Now I had to fulfill those orders after promising to do so in three weeks. My start-up company—which was just me—teetered between becoming a massive success and a massive failure right out of the gate.

The pressure was getting to me. I had eight different social media accounts to handle, plus I was the customer service department handling orders, shipping, and constant questions like "Hey, where's my stuff?" I was also filming myself for fitness videos and editing and uploading them.[1]

I coped in several ways. The first was by working more and sleeping less—way less. I'd push myself until two or three in the morning, sleep for three or four hours, and then get at it again. Once a week, I'd pull an all-nighter, which reminded me of finals week at the University of Illinois.

When I retired from the NFL, I thought Adderall—used to treat

---

1 As I fell further behind, I had to refund half that money because I couldn't handle all the orders.

those with ADHD like me—would help me as an entrepreneur, so I got a prescription and took the pills. To keep me charging hard, I would up my dosage occasionally.

I'd often be too wired to sleep, so I started smoking weed, which helped to bring me down with all the stimulants in my system. This created a cycle where I woke up each morning in a fog feeling like hot garbage, which had me reaching for the bottle of Adderall to fire up the engines to give me motivation to get going. I began taking more Adderall throughout the day and smoking more and more weed in the evening. My highs got higher, and my lows got lower.

I was an emotional wreck. On the bright side, my business was blowing up. To deal with all the swirling emotions, I thought adding Percocet, a painkiller, to the mix would be a great idea.

I'd go to the doctor complaining of chronic pain in my back—which was true—and walk out of the examination room with a three-month prescription for Percocet or some other super-potent oxycodone painkiller. When I would chew these up and the 30-milligram blue pills hit the bloodstream, it felt like I was getting a hug from Jesus. But the more pills I swallowed, the less special I felt.

After about a year of this, I was taking the painkillers just to feel okay. But hey, my supplement company was making me money. Too bad my marriage was falling apart. Bottom line: I was "successfully" spiraling into a deep depression. What a sad, lonely, and pathetic life I was living.

This trio of powerful drugs produced changes in my demeanor. I was super irritable and short-tempered with the kids, and I stopped taking Laura out on our weekly date night. Any hint of romance between us was just a flicker; we passed each other like ships in the night. And when my wife wasn't available, guess who I turned to?

The always willing, always available pornhub.com. And to be very honest with you, I actually paid $14.99 a month for "premium access" to the private content. Instead of watching porn in 1080p resolution, I decided to invest in myself because I enjoyed watching my X-rated smut in high-def 4k.

In many ways, porn had been a part of my life for a long time. In season or out of season, I'd go to the porn well two or three times a week. After retiring from pro football, these sessions happened late at night—or when Laura wasn't in the house. I made sure to hide this dirty little secret from her.

I knew porn wasn't good for me, but whenever I was feeling down, porn was there. Whenever I felt despair, porn was there. Whenever I felt rejected, porn was there. Even when I wanted to celebrate, porn was there. I built a love/hate relationship with porn, knowing that I shouldn't go there, but just like the drugs, the fireworks that set off in my brain scratched the itch. I justified it as the lesser of two evils. *At least I'm not cheating.*

If you look at me in totality, I was a father of four who was abusing drugs, ignoring my responsibilities as a dad, ignoring my marriage, and habitually watching porn. Things got so bad between Laura and me that I told her I needed a break. I went on Airbnb, found a studio apartment above someone's garage for $79 a day, and moved out for a week before coming to my senses and limping back home.

I was seriously messed up and didn't know what to do.

The business coach I was working with to help grow my supplement company only gave me direction in the financial pillar of my life. I was used to being coached, so I took his direction to the nth degree and put my blinders on across all other areas of my life. I failed to realize that my work obsession pushed my family away from me, which was the exact opposite reason why I was working so hard in the first place—to provide for them.

I share this story because while my business coach helped

me scale my business, he coached me in such a way that he blew up the rest of my life. I didn't have the foresight to recognize this because I thought wealth would be my legacy. I desperately needed a change, a shift toward grace and not grind. I needed a legacy filled with deep faith and strong relationships, not just a bunch of trophies and a fat bank account.

I learned that focusing on *one* area of excellence created gaps in other areas of my life. I got off the hamster wheel and regained a grip at home by aligning with the right mentors—well-rounded individuals who created fruit in multiple areas. Mentors who had healthy businesses, bodies, and relationships.

When I moved back home, I was happy Laura hadn't changed the locks, but she wasn't exactly standing there with open arms. We were always in love, but I wasn't well and needed to get right.

As we rebuilt our marriage, I reflected on my collegiate days as a decathlete. I wasn't the best at each event, but I was the best across all events. You see, you don't have to win any of the disciplines, but you do have to show up for every single one of the ten events. I'd seen some of the most talented decathletes blow a championship title because they failed to show up for the first event on the second day of competition. It didn't matter if you got first place in nine events, but if you were a "no show" in one event, you would be disqualified from the competition.

A decathlete champion is crowned from the culmination of points, not a singular event or performance. And I had to be there for every event going on in my life, meaning I couldn't skip out on Laura or my family in any area. I had to be there for them and fight through each of my issues.

A radical encounter with God in the desert in 2018 changed me forever. I was attending a men's conference that my church put on when I definitely felt the touch of the Holy Spirit. A feeling of peace welled in my heart, a peace that surpasses all understanding, which the apostle Paul talks about in Philippians 4:7. (More to come on this in the next chapter.)

After that men's conference, I began to show up as a husband and father in ways I hadn't been in months prior. Slowly but surely, our family and marriage came to a place of healing.

You see, there are roles we choose not to pursue in life because they don't come naturally to us. Instead, we double down on areas that come naturally to us, but I have news for you: you won't be remembered by the ones you love for being the best businessman, best athlete, or best artist. You will, however, be remembered for being the best husband, father, and friend. Life is a relational game, not a transactional one.

So instead of going all-in in one area of life that comes naturally to you, aim for progress, not perfection, in all areas of life—just like a great decathlete. I want you to shift your identity from being a specialist to a well-rounded athlete of life—a man or woman who has gifts but doesn't let weaknesses disqualify him or her from being a world-champion version of themselves.

I realize this can be overwhelming. That's why having the right mentor who keeps you accountable to the mission and vision you set before yourself is crucial.

The best mentor is the teacher who has already walked the path you're on, fought the battles, and made it to the other side. Someone who has seen the fruit of his or her efforts. That mentor can help you from experience, not theory, because champions learn from their mistakes, make adjustments, and make forward progress.

I like what my friend, influencer and poet Billy Alsbrooks, says: "Champions make adjustments, not excuses."

In addition to having a mentor—a Paul—every person who wants to grow should have a Barnabas and a Timothy in their life.

Let's start with the apostle **Paul**, who exemplified a successful mentor relationship with Timothy. Paul carefully selected Timothy to work with him in ministry, equipped him for ministerial tasks, placed him in a challenging work environment, communicated the value of their relationship, and empowered him for success.

Barnabas was an early church leader who showed us how a friend can be closer than a brother. He was an encourager and kept others accountable, but he accepted them at their reality while holding them to their ideals.

And lastly, **Timothy**, the protégé of Paul. He showed us what devotion and service to others look like and how our inadequacies and inabilities should not keep us from being available to God. Youthfulness need not be an excuse for ineffectiveness.

While you can make progress on your own, the right tribe of mentors will time-collapse your development, identify pitfalls to avoid, and make sure you stay on track to achieve your goals in the most efficient manner.

Think of the piano, for example, which has eighty-eight keys. Under the piano lid lies eighty-eight different piano wires that must be precisely tuned to an exact pound per square inch, or PSI, to achieve the desired note or tone. The average tension required in each piano wire is 168 PSI, meaning every piano has 14,784 pounds of strategically adjusted tension necessary for the ideal song to be played.

Coaches are like piano tuners, and I can attest to the importance of coaches helping me "tune" my life through conferences, books, YouTube videos, online courses, Mastermind events, and one-on-one sessions.

Coaches and mentors have played an integral role in every season of my life. They will remain a priority as I grow and evolve into a better version of myself. One of my mentors, Keith Craft, always said, "The *who* you do life with is more important than the *what* you do because the *who* you do life with ultimately determines *what* you do in life."

Here's an exercise for you:

Write down who your Paul, Barnabas, and Timothy are:

- Paul:

- Barnabas:

- Timothy:

If you don't have a Paul, Barnabas, and Timothy in your life, you need to get to work! These relationships are imperative for you to become the decathlete of your life.

7
RELATIONSHIP, NOT RELIGION

ONE OF THE MOST EXCITING days of my life was when I turned sixteen and got my driver's license and my first car... freedom! My first wheels were a 1986 Cadillac Fleetwood Brougham. I loved this car!

My dad bought the Caddy off an older friend who was going blind; he paid $3,000. Even though my new car was really twelve years old, the vehicle hadn't been driven much and was in mint condition. I washed and waxed this beauty twice a week, making sure I shined the tires with Armor All so I'd be wheels up for the weekends with the boys, going from house party to remote cornfield keggers.

I paid for all this partying and gas with money I saved up from my summer work as a YMCA camp counselor and lifeguard at the Deming Dipper, a municipal pool. I used my paychecks and birthday money to purchase big three-inch whitewall tires, custom rims for my land yacht, and a CD player. My Fleetwood was the car all my friends wanted to ride in because it was about twenty feet long with lots of legroom. The cushion leather seats were better than a La-Z-Boy.

In previous chapters, I shared a little about how my dad was "old school." Let me elaborate more on that. My dad raised the three of us to be the same, and he wasn't one to accept excuses from us. What I mean is that if we made a mistake, we received a punishment. If we broke the rules, we paid the price. My dad was firm and fair.

A lot of the time, I was scared of what was gonna happen when I had to face my dad, so I did my best to hide things from him. I learned that if my dad didn't know about it, I wouldn't get punished for my crime.

I relate this to say I grew up viewing God in a similar manner. I regarded Him as a white-haired man sitting on a throne, watching and waiting to punish me for my wicked, evil ways.

So, consider what happened after I wrecked my Cadillac within six months of my sixteenth birthday. I will never forget the crunch of the metal I heard when I made an illegal U-turn and got smacked. Luckily, I didn't get a scratch. The Fleetwood? Not so good. I remember thinking, *I have to call Dad, but he's going to freaking kill me!*

This is like the difference between religion and relationship. *Religion* is making a mistake and wanting to hide what happened from your dad because you're sure he's going to punish you.

Having a *relationship* means that as soon as you hear the crunch of the metal and realize what you've done, you're thinking, *I gotta call my dad. He'll help me. He'll tell me exactly what to do.*

In a similar vein, religion with Jesus never saves anyone. Religion never results in any cures. Religion never remasters identities or restores marriages.

Instead, God desires us to have a relationship with Him where we can call on Him anytime, even when we've wrecked the car.

I was thirty-six years old when I got into a relationship with Jesus, and that's when things started to shift. I stopped playing defense against God and started playing offense with God.

About two weeks after arriving in San Diego from New Jersey, as we were unboxing our family of seven and counting—Laura was pregnant again—we got an invite to a birthday party.

While there, I met a guy named Ash. We talked for over an hour and got along well. I felt like I made a new friend. Before we left the party, he invited me to his church, which was called Awaken.

I'll be honest: we hadn't been to church in a long time, but something about Ash's invitation told me we should check it out. Plus, I knew God was what I needed. On that first Sunday morning, Laura and I dropped our kids off at kids' church and then snuck into the last row in the most dimly lit pair of seats, five minutes late because I didn't want to be recognized or engage in any awkward conversations with any "churchy" people. Laura and I sat and settled in to watch, listen, and absorb.

A couple of worship songs happened. I saw people raising their hands, crying, laughing, and singing their praise to God. They didn't care what people thought of them. But everything seemed genuine and real. As a window shopper, I was watching intently.

Then one of the pastors, Dr. Matt Hubbard, came on stage to preach. About two minutes into his message, there was an awkward pause when he stopped and looked at the top left corner of the auditorium. I froze when he pointed in my direction and said: "I feel an overwhelming prompting from the Holy Spirit to tell you something."

Initially, I didn't believe he was talking to me, so I turned around to see who he was speaking to, but the only thing behind me was a wall. Then the pastor said again, "I'm talking to you . . . yes, you!"

Now the spotlight was pointing at me with more than four hundred church-going folks staring in my direction.

"God is telling me that you've been gone for a long time," Dr. Hubbard continued. "And He wants you to know you're home now. And He's going to heal your situation." The pastor continued to go on for over a minute, speaking exactly into my situation and suffering.

I was dumbfounded—and my mind was racing.

I thought I was gonna slide into this church and slide out unnoticed . . . hahaha. God was like *NOT UP IN HERE!* Or more delicately put:

> *Hey, Weatherford. I got a message for you. I'm gonna grab your attention in grand fashion, and I'm gonna use another man to speak directly into you.*

I was also thinking, *How did this pastor guy know these things about me?*

I didn't have an answer, but my first experience at this church was unlike any other church I had experienced before. The spiritual energy was different, and the people inside Awaken seemed unchained. I was intrigued but still skeptical.

I think it's important to mention my experience with church as a kid. Church was very strict. Very regimented. Everyone needed to wear khaki pants and tuck their shirts in. I heard a lot about the fires of hell, don't have sex until marriage, don't break any of the Ten Commandments, follow the rules, and religion means being a follower of Jesus.

I felt so much shame and guilt growing up in the church. I didn't see powerful men on Sunday mornings. I saw overweight, undisciplined, khaki-wearing Christians who didn't want to be there, but you could tell church was important to their wives.

My childhood church spoke about God and Jesus a lot, but the pastors didn't mention the Holy Spirit very often. I say that because—until I attended Awaken Church— I had never felt the presence of the Holy Spirit in my life. What I felt when I walked into Awaken was an overwhelming sense of peace and joy. I didn't know exactly what this energy was, but it was intoxicating to watch people worship in the presence of that incredible power and might.

So, let me simplify this.

Most of us have heard of the Holy Trinity—the Father, Son, and Holy Spirit. But what is the role and function of each?

God the Father created the heavens and the earth and all of creation. He is the beginning and the end.

His Son, Jesus, was sent by God to destroy the works of the devil. He never sinned and paid the price of our sins by dying on the cross and defeating death. After Jesus rose from the grave (Easter), He sat with his disciples and told them over a meal that he was going to heaven soon to be at the right hand of the Heavenly Father. When the disciples heard this, they freaked out, saying, "No, Jesus! Don't leave us. What will we do without You?"

Before His death, Jesus told the disciples:

> "And I will ask the Father, and he will give you another Advocate, who will never leave you. He is the Holy Spirit, who leads into all truth."
>
> John 14:12 (NLT)

After Jesus was resurrected and ascended into heaven, all His followers gathered in a place called the Upper Room. They waited and prayed, and after ten days, Scripture says, suddenly, a sound like rushing wind filled the room, and tongues of fire appeared on each of them. The disciples were filled with the Holy Spirit and began speaking in different languages when they preached. This attracted a crowd in Jerusalem, and Peter explained that the outpouring of the Holy Spirit was a fulfillment of prophecy.

Many were convicted, repented, and were baptized. This marked the birth of the early Christian church, empowered by the Holy Spirit to spread the message of salvation. (You can learn more about the Holy Spirit in the book of Acts, which will give you even more context for how alive, real, and active the Holy Spirit is.)

Now that your Bible lesson is complete, let me turn back to Awaken Church, which was my first experience with a Spirit-filled congregation. Without me realizing it, I experienced a small dose of the Holy Spirit when I walked into Awaken for the first time.

I started returning every Sunday with my family after that because I knew I wasn't leading myself, my marriage, and my family the way God was calling me to. Every time I stepped into this church, it felt like I was taking a spiritual shower. Every service refreshed my spirit and gave me hope for my current situation.

My hunger and thirst for more was growing. I found my way into a weekly men's prayer group that met every Tuesday morning at 5:30 a.m. These men were not your buttoned-down, khaki-wearing Christians. They were fifty guys from all walks of life—business owners, athletes, musicians, creators, and leaders. They were strong and vulnerable at the same time. It was in this room that I learned and experienced the power of vulnerability. It was in this room that I learned the power of prayer and how God uses other men to walk us into freedom through confession and repentance.

I experienced firsthand the power of this Scripture:

> Therefore confess your sins to each other and pray for each other so that you may be healed. The prayer of a righteous person is powerful and effective.
>
> JAMES 5:16 (NIV)

I needed to be around men who didn't need anything from me but wanted to love me into being my best. This place of worship taught me the difference between religion and relationship.

After six months of consistently attending church and men's prayer, I got invited to the Emerge men's conference hosted by Awaken. Imagine 2,500 men gathering for three days and two nights in high desert country east of San Diego. If you've read this book passively up to this point, it's time to lean in because this is when it gets good.

I got special permission from Dr. Hubbard to bring my eleven-year-old son Ace to this men's event since it was supposed to be for those thirteen and up. Upon arrival, Ace and I were given two-foot-long wooden 2x4s with two holes and a string. A guy said, "Here's your burden, and here's your Sharpie marker."

We were instructed to write down all of our burdens on the 2x4 and wear the wooden plank on our backs all weekend, not to embarrass us but to remind us again and again how burdens affect all that we do.

When the first evening of Emerge came, we all headed under a giant circus tent for the last event. I sat midway back with Ace and my friend Nick Unsworth, who invited me to the men's conference.

My anticipation was high. I had not seen so many men worshiping at once. The extreme energy from 2,500 sober men for God was a new thing for me. Then, it was time for the main speaker to come up. Our fierce leader, Pastor Jurgen, announced his name, but it went right over my head. I noticed, though, that the speaker didn't use the stairs. Instead, he jumped up on the stage at six foot six, 280 pounds, with twenty-inch arms and hair as white as Bob Barker since he looked to be in his late fifties. He instantly garnered my respect because I could tell this guy was like me—a lifelong iron addict.

I could also tell that he was not your typical preacher. The next moment changed my life as he spoke into the microphone. I felt like a lightning bolt of heat hit my body. My skin started to vibrate. *What is happening to me?*

I felt like I was levitating out of my chair. I felt really, really high, but not impaired. I looked to my left to see if my friend Nick was also floating in a euphoric state of confusion with me.

As I looked over, Nick was picking the dirt and dust of the desert out of his nose. I could clearly see he was not experiencing what I was, so I asked, "Hey, Nick. What's this guy's name?"

He looked at the conference program and whispered, "His name is Keith Craft. Says he's a pastor in Texas."

I didn't recognize the name, so I pulled out my phone and typed in *Keith Craft*. The third image that popped up was a picture of this guy with a mullet from the 1990s breaking a stack of concrete blocks with a chop of his right hand. I was still vibrating and thought, *Is this the guy from Baton Rouge back when I was eleven? At the Power Team event at Comite Baptist Church? It can't be . . .*

I watched intently as he continued to give a riveting forty-minute keynote . . . pacing up and down the stage like a lion.

When Keith Craft finished, I sprinted around the crowd to

the side of the stage because I needed to tell him that he changed my life when I was eleven years old, that he showed a young kid a world of possibility and gave me permission to be successful, strong, bold, loving, outspoken, and excellent. And not only did he give me permission, but he also gave me a picture of what a godly man was supposed to look like.

When I got to the side of the stage, I vomited my entire Wikipedia of achievements to this pastor to help him understand how profoundly his ministry had impacted the man I had become. He listened, smiled, and thanked me for telling him. As I began to walk back to my chair, my skin was still vibrating; I felt like I was walking on clouds. I could barely feel my feet and knew at that moment God was real, that God was good, and that He was operating outside of time in that moment I was in.

I found my way back to my seat and sat next to my friend Nick. "You're never going to believe this," I began.

Then I realized my son wasn't around.

"Where's Ace?"

"Beats me. I thought he was with you."

I began to panic, fearing I lost my son in a tent full of thousands of strangers.

Nick held up his hand and pointed toward the stage. "Looks like your son is up at the front receiving Jesus. Look..."

I turned toward the stage. Among an ocean of grown men, I saw my firstborn praying with Keith Craft—the same pastor who had led me to Jesus twenty-five years earlier. Mind blown!!!

I'll pause right here.

As you are reading my story, you're probably thinking, *Could this really be real?* The answer is yes. It happened. God is real. He loves you. He has a plan for your life. But my total breakthrough was not in that moment. I still had porn, pills, procrastination, lust, and loneliness written as burdens on the block of wood still strapped to my back. So even though I realized God was real, that still didn't change the fact that I had unresolved problems, addictions, and issues.

The Emerge conference ended with a massive bonfire. Every group of forty men had two team leaders. Each leader prayed a short and powerful prayer while they placed their hands on each man's burdens before the guy released them into the billowing fire.

Jesus talked about the power of praying together in Matthew 18:19 (NIV):

> "Again, truly I tell you that if two of you on earth agree about anything they ask for, it will be done for them by my Father in heaven."

When I encountered the Holy Spirit in the tent the night before, I knew God was real and that He was good. I desperately wanted Him to take these burdens away from me. I remember my prayer that night as I stood before the bonfire:

> "God, I need more of you and less of me. God, I repent of my sins. I ask for Your forgiveness. I invite Jesus into my heart to be my Lord and Savior. I pray Your Holy Spirit will fill me, lead me, strengthen me, and guide me. I pray You take from me what I can't handle . . . all of the burdens. I release them in Jesus' name."

I watched my 2x4 burn in the blaze and knew He would answer my prayer. I went home from this event changed by God. I had gone into the desert, where I encountered the Spirit of God. I released my burdens, and I rededicated my life to Christ.

RELATIONSHIP, NOT RELIGION

Two things in life are important for you to do: Give God something to work with and give men something to respect.

I knew before this conference that I didn't respect myself because I didn't honor myself, my mind, or my body. I was led by my flesh.

I was dishonoring myself, my wife, and my family with some of the habits and relationships that I allowed to be part of my life. After this event, I took out the samurai sword and cut them off. Especially porn.

I started by repenting to Laura as soon as I got home. She knew porn existed in my life, but she had no idea how much that gunk was robbing the emotional and physical intimacy that God had waiting for us. That night, I enrolled her in partnering with me to slay this giant together.

She said yes, and I have never watched porn again, for which I rejoice in Jesus' name.

So let me ask you a few questions:

    What burdens are you carrying?

    Who have you not forgiven?

    Have you not forgiven yourself?

    Why aren't you giving it all to God?

What broken belief systems, traumatic experiences, depression, anxiety, perfectionism, procrastination, lust, what addictions, shame, guilt, or labels are you carrying that were never meant for you to carry?

Maybe it was an experience of failure as a kid that has limited you as an adult. Or perhaps it was a teacher who told you that you were stupid. Comments like this may seem insignificant to an adult, but to children, hearing those words can flip their world upside down until they choose to bring them to the light and release them.

I want you to identify your burden right now. Use the next page to write down all the burdens you're carrying that you want God to take away from you.

I'll give you some of my burdens to help you prime your pump to purge. I wrote down these at the Emerge conference:

- depression
- anxiety
- imposter syndrome
- lust
- porn
- pills
- perfectionism
- procrastination
- shame
- guilt
- addictions
- dirtiness
- perversion
- worthlessness
- soul ties with past sexual partners
- suicidal thoughts
- unforgiveness for others and myself

After you write yours down, ask yourself:
Do I want to lay these down?
Do I want total freedom?

Of course, you do. Now pray and ask God to remove these burdens from your life once and for all. And as you pray, speak from your heart.

RELATIONSHIP, NOT RELIGION

Write Your Burdens Here

After writing down your burdens, tear out this page and light a match to it!

8
WISE MEN TAKE BATHS

I LOVE THIS QUOTE FROM ABRAHAM Lincoln, the 16th President of the United States, because of the way it speaks to the importance of planning, preparation, and timing:

> "Give me six hours to chop down a tree, and I will spend the first four sharpening the axe."

Before I encountered God in the desert, my entire life was about doing and achieving. I spent very little time being still or thinking or praying about anything. I was trying to cash checks and snap necks. My philosophy could be summed up in this manner: "Ain't nobody got time for praying . . . I'll leave that to the wives and pastors."

In this chapter, I'm going to teach you how you can spend less time being busy and more time being productive. I'm going to teach you how to get more of God's wisdom, peace, and protection in your life. I'll teach you how to pray a specific prayer to activate a supernatural covering over your life, family, and finances. Finally, I'm going to take you into the supernatural realm and help you get aware of what's really going on here on Earth.

You'll learn how and when you need to talk to God and what to ask for.

After Emerge, many things shifted in my life, especially my mindset, my habits, my marriage, my self-worth, my identity, how I invested my time, and who I invested time with. I am believing that if you're reading these words I'm writing, that means you have already asked God to forgive you of your sin, just like I did. I am also believing you have invited Jesus into your heart, maybe even for the first time.

But maybe you have a question like this:

So Steve, how do you make sure the decisions you make truly create permanent change in your life?

I'm glad you asked. Here's my answer: Take a bath.

"Wait. What?"

No, not a cold bath or an ice bath, which I'm a big fan of. I'm talking about an ordinary warm bath every morning, and you don't need to do Wim Hof breathing either. I just want you to sit, soak, be still, and pray. Seems counterproductive to making progress, right?

For the first thirty-six years of my life, my entire self-worth was tied up in my to-do list. I decided to flip the game on its head and make my life about a "to-be" list, not a to-do list. I knew that according to Scripture, God wasn't impressed with any of my "works," but He was obsessed with who I was. So, I decided to focus my life on my "being" instead of "doing."

Part of my routine change wasn't just about creating newness. This morning routine I came up with was a biblical way of equipping myself to be mentally, physically, and spiritually ready for every "to do" on my list.

When you equip yourself this way, you will have more wisdom, less fear, more peace, and fewer feelings of being overwhelmed. You will also have a renewed spiritual covering that will protect you against the enemy's attacks.

Yes, I'm referring to demons. Most people don't like to talk about them because they make them nervous, but I'm not most people.

Woah, Steve, hold up here. You're getting religious on me.

I hear you, but it's time to keep reading so I can explain further. Can we agree God is real?

Sure, Steve.

If God is real, can we agree the devil is real?

I guess so.

Can we agree that there are angels?

Sure.

So then can we agree that demons exist?

I'm listening.

I hope you're still with me because the fact that you know all of that—and you're likely walking around without a specific protective covering guaranteed to you from your Heavenly Father—means you have to equip yourself daily with specific prayer, something like this:

> God, I have sinned. I'll probably sin today. I'm incomplete without You. Please forgive me.

RE-RECEIVE Jesus every morning. You don't need Jesus one day; you need Him every day. Ask Him to heal your heart and renew your mind to think and love like Him.

Use this morning prayer time to **RELEASE** any more burdens in your life. Give your junk to Jesus. Let Him handle what's heavy on your heart.

Be sure to ask the Holy Spirit to fill you. Ask the Holy Spirit to guide you, strengthen you, convict you, and comfort you. Ask the Holy Spirit and go before you in your day.

And lastly, you must "**ROBE UP**," meaning put on the armor of God as you go about your day.

If putting on the armor of God is a new idea for you, no wonder the enemy has been kicking your teeth in. No wonder you feel like a weak Christian. You're trying to defeat darkness with your flesh and good intentions, but all that ends up doing is making you a walking target for the great accuser.

Get familiar with your weapons. Each has a different role and function.

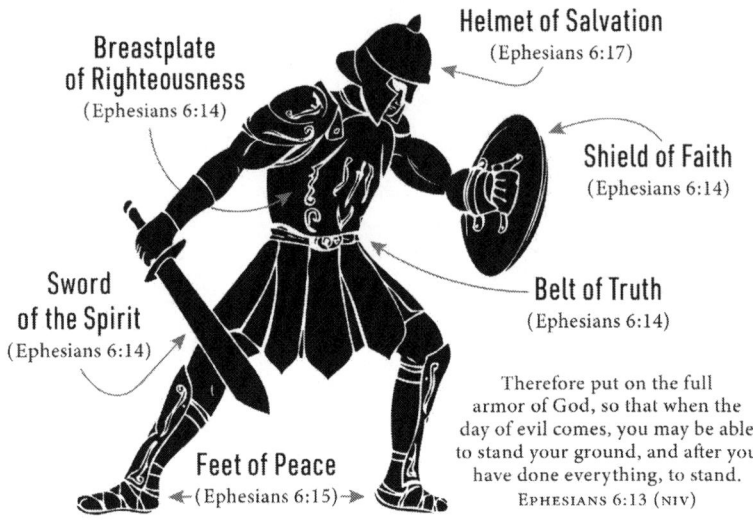

Therefore put on the full armor of God, so that when the day of evil comes, you may be able to stand your ground, and after you have done everything, to stand.
EPHESIANS 6:13 (NIV)

All of this seems a little extreme, Steve...

Thanks for being honest with me, but let me break down how God works for you with an analogy.

Have you ever taken your kids to Chuck E. Cheese or Dave & Busters?

Our family loves arcades like you find at Dave & Busters. My four girls, especially, love collecting tickets to redeem for toys, candy, and girly things. My oldest son, Ace, spends a lot of time on the hoop shot, football toss, or shooting games. And my youngest, Kingston, doesn't need tokens at all. All my preschooler wants to do is sit inside every driving game, every roller-coaster ride, or every motorcycle game and pretend to play.

I have six kids with a large range of ages. Some of my kids are mature and trustworthy, and some of my kids have juvenile delinquent tendencies. No matter their age, I want them to stay near to me. So how do I allow my family to enjoy what the arcade has to offer while keeping them close?

I give them only enough game tokens to be gone for a short while. I want them to come back to me for more tokens so I can give them instruction, protection, and provision.

This is exactly how I want you to view your relationship with God. He doesn't want you gone all week until the next Sunday morning. He wants you to be close to Him every day, especially every morning as you get going with your day. He wants you to come to Him for provision, protection, and direction before you do anything else. It's like He gives you just enough tokens to last the day. When you approach Him in prayer the following morning, you will receive your next set of tokens.

This is what your morning can look like:

Start your day with a warm bath. Listen to some low-level worship music while you soak in the calming water. Use this time to close your eyes and pray. Here's a prayer I love to say during my morning bath time:

> God, I need more of you and less of me. Lord God, I repent of my sins. I ask for Your forgiveness. I invite Jesus into my heart to be my Lord and Savior.
>
> I pray your Holy Spirit will fill me, lead me, strengthen me, and guide me. I pray You take from me what I can't handle. Take all of the burdens. I release them now. I put on the armor of God and pray that it would protect me from any attack or snare

from the enemy.

I pray these things in the mighty name of Jesus, amen.

Of course, you don't have to listen to worship music and pray this prayer while you're soaking in a bathtub. You can take this time to pray and reflect while lying in bed before you get up or cozying up on the couch after the kids leave for school. You can listen and pray during your morning commute. If you work at home, you can spend ten or fifteen minutes listening to worship music and reading God's Word before praying at the start of your workday.

The important thing here is to create time to **RE-RECEIVE** Jesus every morning, **RELEASE** your burdens to Him, and **ROBE UP** with his mighty armor so you can fight off any evil that comes your way.

9

IT'S TIME TO GO PRO

Now that you've laid down your burdens and know how to start your every day, it's time to talk about how we're gonna operate. And the only way to get there is to restore order and get clear on your commitments.

Here's the deal:

Amateurs make decisions based on their feelings. Pros make decisions based on their commitments. When an amateur athlete's alarm clock goes off at 5 a.m., he hits the snooze button. He either falls back asleep straight away or thinks about whether he needs more sleep. If he's still half-awake, he might mentally do a body scan for any sore spots or think about what the rest of his day looks like. At the end of his checklist, he decides if he "feels" like getting up, taking action, and doing what is required, not desired.

When an elite athlete wakes up in the morning, however, he doesn't think, he doesn't scan anything, and he doesn't negotiate. He gets out of bed right away because his commitment to an early-morning workout was pre-decided.

I want to help you pre-decide who you are and what matters most to you so when the alarm clock of adversity hits—and it will—you'll be ready. I want to help you stand firm in commitments, not your fleshly feelings.

So, let me begin with a couple of questions:

- How many times have you made an emotional decision and regretted it later?
- How many times have you decided to honor your commitment but regretted it later?

I bet the number of times you regretted bailing out on your commitments is a whole lot shorter. Here's the fact of the matter: when it comes to living a championship life, there are a few non-negotiables.

In this chapter, you will learn how to tame your tongue and speak like a champion. You will learn how to create with the voice God gave you (and not curse) and also learn how to live with a new operating system.

I'm going to teach you how to do something you've probably never done consistently, and you'll be proud of yourself when you learn how to *go pro!*

Championship language is how champions speak to themselves. It's how the elite operates and why they are successful. I'll start by sharing the most powerful phrase on this planet: *I am (fill in the blank.)*

Some examples:

I am organized.
I am a mess.
I am strong.
I am weak.

There is strength and power in our words, and they shape our lives and how we think of ourselves. Our words come from our speech, and our speech comes from our tongue. Let me share a short story from a Navy SEAL buddy of mine to give you a better understanding of what I am talking about. One time, my buddy said he was on a mission to stop a giant container ship from taking supplies to another area. He had to go underwater to stop the ship from arriving at its destination, so he swam a mile underwater to the ship's hull.

When he got there, he realized how massive the ship's side was. The hull was super thick, so he knew the explosives he brought along wouldn't blow a hole in the side. At that moment, he determined he needed another solution. After considering his options, he decided to attach the explosives to the ship's rudder, thinking that if he could damage the rudder with a blast, the container ship couldn't stay on course and therefore wouldn't be able to get to where it was supposed to go.

You see, the way you speak can get you to your destination, or it can blow up your entire mission. The devil doesn't have to sink you. He just has to distract you enough to get you off course and stop you from getting where you're trying to go. Another way to put this is that death and life are in the power of the tongue.

Your tongue is your rudder—it's what controls you and decides what direction you will go, as the apostle James wrote:

> And a small rudder makes a huge ship turn
> wherever the pilot chooses to go, even though
> the winds are strong. In the same way, the tongue
> is a small thing that makes grand speeches.
> But a tiny spark can set a great forest on fire.
> JAMES 3:4-5 (NLT)

The enemy doesn't need to destroy you or sink your ship. All he needs to do is to bust your rudder and remove your ability to course-correct your way. When we don't tame the tongue, it runs wild . . . it gossips, it curses, it discourages, it judges . . . it easily leads us astray:

> But no human being can tame the tongue. It
> is restless and evil, full of deadly poison.
> JAMES 3:8 (NLT)

Okay, Steve. I believe you. My tongue needs to be tamed. I acknowledge it can lead me astray. How do I do this?

It begins with taking words out of your mouth and never speaking them again. I'm talking about words of weakness, words of doubt, words of confusion, and even words about death. Words like "I hope," "I can't," "I'll try" —remove them! Words of hesitation imply a lack of confidence or belief. And if you really believe that Jesus is your Big Brother, you would talk differently and speak with ridiculous confidence . . . because you know your Big Brother has your back.

Mighty men and women of God don't speak from a position of weakness. They don't use words like *can't* because *can't* speaks to the inability to overcome. As a man or woman of God, we don't accept that. So, I want you to shift your language from "I'm hoping this will happen" to "I am believing this will happen."

Weak language: "I'm trying to finish a marathon."

Champion language: "I'm training to finish a marathon."

We don't "try" either. Trying is for weak people, and you are not weak. Your language should reflect your identity and strength. The famous philosopher and Jedi Master Yoda once said, "Do, or do not . . . there is no try."

Trying implies that failure is an option. Champions don't fail. They win, or they learn, but they never fail.

I love these Scriptures, and you should too:

- Philippians 4:13 (NLT) says we can do all things through Christ.
- Ephesians 4:29 (NIV) says, "Do not let any unwholesome talk come out of your mouths, but only what is helpful for building others up according to their needs, that it may benefit those who listen."

My objective in this chapter is for you to be more than mindful of what you speak. Your words have the ability to shift the atmosphere in every space you go. I've been guilty of raising my voice and using words that hurt. I've seen how my shift in language—or the way I say certain things—has changed my home. I've made it my goal not to let words come out of my mouth that don't give life, love, encouragement, honor, or something constructive to the situation. If I make a mistake in my words, I quickly adjust myself and take responsibility to be better.

One thing that truly helped me to clean up not just my language but my mind (that is if you really want the smoke . . . if you truly want your mind to be fully reconditioned by goodness, grace, mercy, power, and love . . .) is to listen to nothing by worship music for an entire year.

One of the reasons you might have difficulty with your language isn't because you're a low-life scumbag but rather because it's the direct result of what you are feeding your mind. Your words are like your physique; if you eat healthy when people are around but pig out on junk late at night, your physique will show. Your body will snitch on you.

The same thing goes for our minds. If we load up our minds with secular music and popular movies that glorify money, power, sex, drugs, and things of the world—but want righteousness to come out to those around us—who are we kidding? What flows from the mind impacts the heart. This is why God's Word teaches us this:

> Above all else, guard your heart, for
> everything you do flows from it.
> PROVERBS 4:23 (NIV)

I challenge you to completely revamp what you put into your mind so that you can change your heart. Don't forget that you can be a thermometer or a thermostat (like my good buddy Ed Mylett says), meaning you can acclimate to whatever is around you and conform to your surroundings. Or you can shift the space. With intentional words, you become the thermostat in the room. You set the temperature and influence of the room and the energy in it by creating, encouraging, and lifting others up with your words.

Now that you got your mouth right and your heart right (with Jesus), it's time to get your mind right, and that's done by the renewing of your mind, which we're called to do in Scripture:

> Do not conform to the pattern of this world, but
> be transformed by the renewing of your mind.
> ROMANS 12:2 (NIV)

I want to help you renew your mind by guiding you through a process of creating a new "operating system" to run your mind.

Imagine buying a brand-new laptop that is powerful and capable, just like you. A laptop can help you create, can help you connect with others, and can help you solve problems.

But one of the first things you have to do before your laptop can do any of those great things is download an operating system that controls and guides the computer. This operating system will be the filter you run all the words and actions through.

I call this operating system the Declaration of Independence, which is the declarative statement that you speak over yourself and is composed of your core values—the traits you want to embody your life.

Let me show you what that looks like by sharing my Declaration of Independence:

> My name is Steve Weatherford. I am a man of integrity, honor, and accountability. I am a son and a warrior of the One Most High . . .

I speak this over myself every morning while I brush my teeth. I do this because I want to re-remind myself what the goal of the day is: be a man of integrity, a man of honor, a man of accountability, and to make my life about God and others around me.

I want to share with you why I chose these traits, what the words actually mean to me, and how they show up in my life.

The first core value I chose to help me lead myself best is **integrity**. To me, integrity means being who you are regardless of who's around. Integrity means living your life for an audience of One. It means the only opinion that matters is God's. It means telling the fear of man and the fear of failure to go to hell.

At the end of the day—even if everyone on this planet rejected me—I would feel peace and joy in knowing that God approves of me. God sees my heart for Him and hears my prayers of desperation. Whom shall I fear if the Lord is in my corner? Because if Jesus lives in my heart, I know I have been adopted as one of God's children, which makes me a co-heir to His promises.

The next core value I chose to lead with my words and actions is **honor** because I knew unlocking that trait would make my life about God and serving others with what God has given me. In other words, my actions would be a way of honoring Him.

Because of my insecurity, I used to be the type of man who would walk into a room of guys and find a way to compete and be "better" than everyone around me.

Then I finally received all of what Jesus meant for me to have... not just forgiveness, but authority, identity, and purpose. So when Jesus' identity became my identity, I realized I didn't need anything from anyone because I was enough because of Jesus. Actually, I'm more than enough through Christ Jesus.

When that understanding finally set in, I realized I needed to change my entire operating system, which I want to help you do now. My goal is to teach you a whole new way of thinking and making decisions.

My last core value is **accountability**. This refers to the willingness to take responsibility for one's actions, decisions, and behaviors. Accountability involves being answerable to yourself and others for the outcomes and consequences of your actions. Accountability often entails being transparent, owning up to mistakes or shortcomings, and actively working toward improvement or making amends. It is a crucial aspect of personal growth, integrity, and building trust in relationships, both personal and professional.

The last part of my Declaration of Independence was this: "I am a son and a warrior of the One Most High." I'm not saying this to sound more holy or righteous than the next person but to remind myself that I *am* God's son. I am worthy, and so are you.

A little more than five years ago, I decided to go all in on following Jesus. I had been in the "pros"—NFL football—for ten years. Now it was time to go pro in life!

I have learned a lot about what separates the average from the elite, as I mentioned earlier. Pros don't leave any area for their feelings to lead their decisions. Pros stick to the process, which means committing to a plan to improve and hone their craft so that they can compete at the highest level.

I want you to ask yourself:

1. What are three values you have that you love about yourself? Several examples are generosity, grit, and discipline.
2. What are three values that are blocking you from greatness? Several examples are worthiness, grace, and forgiveness.
3. What are three things you love to do with people? Several examples are running, leading, and serving.

Grab a sheet of paper and write down your answers. After you've done that, I want you to spend some time wordsmithing those values and activities to create your own powerful Declaration of Independence.

Feel free to use mine to help guide you in creating yours:

My name is (fill in the blank). I am a man (or a woman) of _____, _____ and _____.

Here is another example from a good friend of mine:

My name is Karlton. I am a disciplined, worthy, and generous servant leader whom God designed to run the race with grace and forgiveness. I give Him all the glory in the story.

Don't just let this be an exercise. Give genuine time, thought, and prayer to the construction of your Declaration of Independence and your "I am" statement. This is the part where what you declare about yourself will make things shift in you so you can shift things around you.

If I can help you get clear on what you're committed to and who you're committed to being, then I firmly believe you can "go pro" in life and get off the hamster wheel of second-guessing yourself. When you know who you are, you'll run in the right direction with confidence.

If you can give God something to work with and offer people something to respect, I believe God can use you and each and every one of us for signs, miracles, and wonders to impact the kingdom.

Let me share a few closing ideas:

- Take some quiet time to identify the core values you want to be known for and that you want to bring into every room. Write them down and then put them in a declarative statement—like a contract with yourself.
- Print out your contract, sign it, and put it somewhere so you can view it every day.
- Take a screenshot of your contract and core values and make it your screen save on your phone.

10

OUTFIT THE LAUNCHPAD WITH YOUR TIME, TALENTS, AND TREASURES

I LIVED SO MUCH OF MY life weighed down by mistakes. I've let the burdens of my addictions, faults, and trauma convince me that I'm uniquely disqualified from God's love, mercy, and forgiveness.

I pray that as you've read through *Wake-Up, Champion*, you haven't just read words on a page but have taken action in between chapters to do the work, pray the prayers, and take back territory from the enemy. I pray that you've already released your burdens fully and completely. I pray that you've received the perfect blood of Christ Jesus into every corner and small space of who you are. God's grace is sufficient through Christ Jesus. He already paid the price, and He would leave the ninety-nine just for you.

So, what are you doing? What's holding you back? Give it up! NOW!

I pray that you've already asked God to forgive you for missing the mark and mishandling your time, talents, and treasures. I pray that you have already asked Jesus into your heart to be your Lord and Savior. I pray that you have already decided what your new core values are.

In this final chapter, I will give you three things I use every day that help me to live a life on brand, on purpose, and on fire for Jesus.

I'll do that by giving you a picture, a compass, and a poem.

The picture is to inspire you.

The tool—a compass—is to lead you.

The poem is to encourage you.

Before I give you the picture, I first want to talk about how practicing visualization has impacted my life and how a good mental picture can help you take your health, wealth, relationships, and legacy to the next level.

I am big on visualization. You have to be to play a position like punter in the NFL. You must have the ability to drop into a Bruce Lee-like Zen focus when the whistle blows before the opening kickoff. You have to make every single punt count. Your mind must be prepared at all times and for all scenarios because you don't get that many chances to jog onto the field when it's fourth down and a punting situation.

On average, NFL teams punt 4.3 times per game. On average, each NFL play is about seven seconds long. Let's do the math: 4.3 x 7 seconds = 30.1 seconds. This means I was on the actual NFL field for thirty seconds out of sixty minutes of playing time. I had very few opportunities to showcase my ability to punt the ball high and deep, and I had a very small margin for error.

I had to train my mind to find maximal focus, relaxation, and execution seven seconds at a time . . . but I also needed to be prepared throughout the entire game, which usually lasts three

OUTFIT THE LAUNCHPAD WITH YOUR TIME, TALENTS, AND TREASURES

hours and twelve minutes in the NFL. One of the tools I used to condition and relax my mind and to help me visualize better was by asking one of the interns on the audiovisual staff to create a highlight reel of all my best punts. I told him I wanted to see my punts from all different angles.

The reason I did this is because I needed to see myself effortlessly executing my skill over and over and over again. I needed to meditate on visualizing myself using all of my strength, size, skill, and athleticism to produce a great punt for my team.

This exercise helped give me a clear picture of what I wanted to have in the future when I was called upon to use my God-given skills, like power and strength, to help my team win the game.

Speaking of skills and talents, when our lifetime is over, each of us will stand before God in judgment. He will review two books with us. The first is the Lamb's Book of Life. If you have truly repented and received Jesus Christ as your Savior and Lord, your name will be written in that book with Jesus' perfect blood, which means your name cannot be removed.

The second book is called the Book of Works, which is what I want to talk to you about. The Book of Works contains everything you did with your time, talents, and treasures. You will stand before God one day, and He will pass judgment based on how much time on earth He gave you, how many talents He put into you, how many treasures He bestowed upon you, and what you did with those talents and treasures. Here is what His Word says about that:

> For we must all appear before the judgment seat of Christ, so that each of us may receive what is due us for the things done while in the body, whether good or bad.
>
> 2 CORINTHIANS 5:10 (NIV)

I imagine reviewing my life with my Heavenly Father will be very similar to how I reviewed the Sunday game film with my coaches and team on Monday mornings. I imagine myself sitting in the film room with a massive eighty-foot screen, just my Heavenly Dad and me. We will watch every single moment of my life together. The bonus is that every mistake of my life will be blotted out by the blood of Jesus. (This will be the first time I'll ever watch a game film that *won't* have any of my mistakes.)

I imagine that as I'm watching this game film, God will have a red-laser pointer just like our head coach Tom Coughlin had when I was on the Giants. Every time I used my time, talents, or treasures to bless, provide, or impact one of God's sons or daughters, I imagine God pausing the game film with a huge smile. I can just see Him pointing the red dot to the screen and telling me why this was such a powerful play for His team.

And then I hope to hear the words that we all want to hear someday from Matthew 25:21 (NIV):

"Well done, good and faithful servant."

Don't you want to look straight at Jesus and hear Him say that to you? This book is designed to help you release all the junk that the enemy has placed on you and step into everything Jesus has for you so you can optimize your time, maximize your talents, and multiply your treasures for the glory of God and the expansion of his kingdom.

Let me coach you up a bit and help you visualize how you will want your meeting to go when you're in heaven's Throne Room. Picture a massive space with shiny floors of gold, rubies, and diamonds and ornately decorated walls and ceiling. Imagine standing in the most beautiful and bright room you've ever seen. Imagine a throne with God sitting in the royal seat, looking at you and smiling as He says, "I'm so glad you're here. Welcome to heaven, but before you go in. I want you to sit on the judgment seat. I want you to see the impact your life had on others."

So where do you want Him to go next?

Do you want Him to show you all the families that were restored as a result of your impact?

Do you want Him to show you all the suicides that were prevented because of your obedience?

Do you want Him to show you how much you maximized every opportunity He gave you?

Do you want Him to show you the generational impact you had on your family because you devoted yourself to God?

The first time I asked myself these questions, I realized for the first thirty-six years of my life, I was using what God gave me to build my own kingdom, which ultimately led to emptiness, depression, anxiety, and no life purpose. So let me make His judgment seat and His "Book of Works" simple for you.

God wants to sit down with you and review three things—your time, talents, and treasures. I want to be clear on this: sitting on the judgment seat won't be a heaven-or-hell meeting; it will be an eternal inheritance meeting.

Based on what you did with those trio of assets in your temporal life will determine what your eternal inheritance will be. The great thing I have learned since I have given it all to God is that this isn't an either/or thing. Living God's way doesn't mean that life sucks and that heaven is great. Living God's way and living the world's way—both are hard.

It's been said that if we pay the right price, we will get paid twice. What does that mean? If we take our time, talents, and treasures and invest them in what matters most to God and not just our own, God will reward us with a better life here on earth and eternal rewards in heaven.

I call that my Kingdom vision, and it's something I think of every day. That is the bull's-eye of my life, the aim of my everyday existence, and the ultimate desire of my heart.

Now that you have a picture, I want to equip you with a tool that contains four promises that I use every day. Just like the visualization I described to you, I grab these promises by using what I call my Warrior Compass.

I've already taught you about putting on the armor of God. Now I want to equip you with a guidance tool. But first, a little background.

I love superheroes, and one of the superheroes that I resonate most with is Batman. Batman didn't have any superpowers, but he did have some super toys. You never knew what Bruce Wayne was going to pull off his yellow utility belt to overcome the enemy.

I want you to imagine yourself as Batman, and one of the tools on your utility belt is the Warrior Compass. I use this compass to keep my eyes fixed on the prize, the target that I just talked to you about. I use this Warrior Compass to walk in radical boldness, joy, peace, and power. When I have the Warrior Compass in my hand, I never retreat, never surrender, and never wave the white flag.

I would imagine that you're wondering what the Warrior Compass looks like:

OUTFIT THE LAUNCHPAD WITH YOUR TIME, TALENTS, AND TREASURES

The Warrior Compass has four cardinal directions. Let me go through each one:

TRUE NORTH

> "But seek first the kingdom and his righteousness,
> and all these things, will be given to you as well."
> MATTHEW 6:33 (NIV)

This is the North Star of the Warrior Compass because in all things and in all situations, a warrior for God should seek first to grow God's kingdom. To do that God's way means doing things in a righteous way.

Seeking first the kingdom of God guides me and keeps me on target while reminding me to make sure that everything I do and the way I do it is about God and for God.

EAST

> Not only so, but we also glory in our sufferings, because we know that suffering produces perseverance; perseverance, character; and character,

> hope. And hope does not put us to shame, because God's love has been poured out into our hearts through the Holy Spirit, who has been given to us.
> Romans 5:3-5 (NIV)

This is my lifetime verse, my X factor. I hang my hat on this Scripture, which is sometimes translated "we rejoice in our sufferings."

If I were to punch the devil in the face with one verse, it would be this one. Not because what the apostle Paul wrote sounds good but because God has proven this verse time and time again.

If you want to grow through everything you go through, BE A REJOICER! And this verse tells you why. Here's the deal: all men and women go through hard things in life. Adversity is inevitable. Some men and women get crushed by those hard things. A smaller percentage are more resilient and become stronger. I want to teach you how to be one of those select few who grow from every situation.

This verse tells us that if we can "pre-decide" to rejoice in all situations, then we will grow our endurance or capacity. Tough times and adversity will also reveal and grow character—and good character is something we all want and money can't buy. As we build character according to this verse, our more durable character can give hope to the people around us. Shouldn't that be a goal of ours—living lives that give inspiration and hope to others?

This verse reminds me of Ronnie Coleman, a professional bodybuilder who captured the Mr. Olympia title for eight consecutive years. Ronnie used to say, "Everyone wants to be a beast—until it is time to do what beasts do."

In other words, everyone wants endurance, everyone wants character, and everyone wants success in whatever they do, but nobody wants to rejoice in the suffering it takes to get there. The enemy wants you to complain, compare your circumstances to others, and play the victim. He knows that if you're complaining, you're not praising. And if you're not praising, you're not growing.

Rejoicing is more than having a positive mindset. It's having a grateful mindset. So when the enemy hits you with hard things, you hit the enemy back with rejoicing.

WEST

> "Have I not commanded you? Be strong
> and courageous. Do not be afraid; do not
> be discouraged, for the Lord your God
> will be with you wherever you go."
> JOSHUA 1:9 (NIV)

This is my reminder that whenever fear rises up, God commands us not to be fearful. It's not a suggestion with Him because He is with me always and wherever I go.

As I guide myself with these promises found from the Warrior Compass, this is the one that gives me boldness and freedom for the way I move and speak. Because when I move, where I move, and where I speak, I know that God is with me, behind me, and for me. So why would I waste any time being afraid or discouraged? When I hit the enemy with rejoicing when I'm suffering, I walk over him with boldness.

SOUTH

> "For I know the plans I have for you," declares
> the Lord, "plans to prosper you and not to harm
> you, plans to give you hope and a future."
> JEREMIAH 29:11 (NIV)

I've shared this verse from Jeremiah 29 before, but it's so key, so fundamental to our Christian walk, that I have to bring it out again. When I think of this direction of the compass, South means retreat. I have strategically placed this promise here because there have been many times when I wanted to quit. There will be more times in the future when I'll want to throw in the towel. When those thoughts creep into my mind—or yours too since setbacks happen to all of us—I am reminded that God has a plan for my life and that God has plans to prosper me and promote me according to this promise.

In essence, Jeremiah 29:11 reminds us that despite the challenges and uncertainties that rain down on us from time to time, God has a solid plan for our lives, a plan filled with hope and a bright future. Let this message of encouragement and reassurance offer comfort and peace in the face of life's storms.

Cling to Him during times of trials and hardships. Find refuge in the Word of God and never give up.

Now that I've given you a picture to inspire you and a tool to lead you, I'm going to finish with a poem to encourage you.

As I just discussed with the Warrior Compass, there's no way to avoid the *hard* in life. The one constant I've realized in the years that God has granted me is that life can and will be hard. At one time, I was focused on building my own world and doing it my way—and that was hard. Then I gave my life 100 percent and completely to Jesus, and that was hard too. There are days when the temptation to give in to what my flesh wants is there. As a matter of fact, it's there every morning when I wake.

I will close by sharing a poem with you that a mentor of mine wrote. I read this poem every single morning of my life to encourage and to re-remind me to want what God wants.

It's a choice we all must make.

CHOOSE YOUR HARD

Being your best is hard
Being your normal is hard

Making wise decisions is hard
Making bad decisions is hard

Being in shape is hard
Being out of shape is hard

Losing weight is hard
Being fat is hard

Working out is hard
Being weak is hard

Being disciplined is hard
Being lazy is hard

Getting out of your comfort zone is hard
Staying in your comfort zone is hard

Starting a business is hard
Working for someone else is hard

Making a lot of money is hard
Making a little bit of money is hard

Being rich is hard
Being poor is hard

Having great relationships is hard
Having bad relationships is hard

Having friends is hard
Having no friends is hard

Fighting for your marriage is hard
Divorce is hard

Having a lot of things is hard

> Having nothing is hard
>
> Living on purpose is hard
> Living off purpose is hard
>
> Doing life God's way is hard
> Doing life your own way is hard
>
> Everything is hard!
>
> —Keith Craft

So let me leave you with this final thought: Wake up, champion! Let's go! God has gifted you with unique talents and treasures to excel in this world well beyond your wildest dreams.

Rise above everything, forgive, love, bring peace to others, and choose hard daily.

IT'S DECISION TIME...

If you're ready to get off the bench and
into the game, scan the QR code.
I want to share a special video message and
pray a special prayer with you.

INVITE STEVE WEATHERFORD TO SPEAK TODAY

Do you want to work with Steve one-on-one or have him activate your audience as a guest speaker at your next event? Then book him today!

Steve Weatherford is a dynamic speaker whose story of redemption has motivated people from all over the world. From his rise to the NFL to his passion for fitness, family, and faith, Steve loves helping entrepreneurs and high achievers find their greatness.

If you would like to book Steve to speak at your event, please contact nextsteps@championsinchristministry.com.